Praying
through
the
Storms
of Life

Devotions & Prayers
for
Difficult Times

BARBOUR
PUBLISHING

Published by Barbour Publishing, Inc., 1810 Barbour Drive, Uhrichsville, Ohio 44683, www.barbourbooks.com.

Our mission is to inspire the world with the life-changing message of the Bible.

Member of the
Evangelical Christian
Publishers Association

Printed in China.

Contents

Introduction.. 5

Abuse.. 6

Accidents 10

Addiction.. 15

Adultery 19

Alcohol Abuse 24

Anger.. 28

Anxiety 33

Bankruptcy 36

Betrayal 40

Challenges.. 44

Chronic Illness... 50

Death of a Child 55

Death of a Parent 59

Death of a Spouse 63

Depression.. 66

Disabilities 71

Disappointment... 76

Dishonesty 81

Divorce/Separation 86

Doubt.. 89

Drug Abuse 93

Dysfunctional Relationships 96

Elderly Parents 101

Enemies 105

Facing Death 110

Failure 114

Family Feuds 118

Family Stress 122

Fear 127

Financial Strain 131

Foreclosure/Eviction 136

Helplessness 139

Hidden Sin 144

Hopelessness 147

Infertility 152

Insomnia 155

Job Loss 158

Job Stress 162

Litigation 166

Prodigal Children 169

Sickness 173

Unforgiveness 176

Violence 180

Worry 183

Introduction

Jesus said, "Here on earth you will have many trials and sorrows." It's a promise: you can expect suffering during your lifetime. Jesus went on to say, "But take heart, because I have overcome the world" (John 16:33 NLT). This is good news, but it doesn't necessarily mean the Lord will quickly resolve any difficulties you encounter.

What He offers is not a problem-free life, but the strength to endure your burdens and overcome your tests. Christians today are not spared many of the griefs that assail humanity—including financial pressures, bankruptcies, dysfunctional relationships, marital breakups, accidents, and diseases. This is why God gave us His Word, "that we through the patience and comfort of the Scriptures might have hope" (Romans 15:4 NKJV).

Praying through the Storms of Life draws from these deep wells of encouragement. It was written to breathe life into you when you are forced to walk a very difficult path. It doesn't offer simplistic answers to serious problems, but it does offer hope—real hope—for your darkest hours.

These devotions and prayers declare boldly that God will never ever forsake you, even when your way seems impossible, your circumstances seem unbearable, and you are most tempted to despair. May you find hope in these pages.

Abuse

Close to His Heart

He tends his flock like a shepherd: he gathers the lambs
in his arms and carries them close to his heart.

ISAIAH 40:11 NIV

When the disciples tried to keep children away from Jesus, He said, "Let the little children come to me" (Mark 10:14 NIV). He then took them in His arms and blessed them. Gathering the lambs in His arms has always been Jesus' way.

But if you have suffered abuse or neglect, gone hungry, or experienced trauma, you may wonder where the Lord was. And where is He now? The Bible assures you: "The LORD is close to the brokenhearted" (Psalm 34:18 NIV). God sees your pain. He loves you and cares deeply for you.

Whatever anyone has done to you, they have done to Jesus (Matthew 25:34–45), so He empathizes with your suffering. "In all their suffering he also suffered" (Isaiah 63:9 NLT). This is one reason Jesus was called "a man of sorrows, and acquainted with grief" (Isaiah 53:3 KJV).

God not only knows when you experience grief, but He also feels your pain and is there to comfort you if you will let Him.

Jesus, I know you are my good shepherd. Teach me to trust You
more. Be my comfort in times of grief and fear. Gather me in
Your loving arms and keep me close to Your heart. Amen.

Recovering from Abuse

"O you afflicted one, tossed with tempest, and not comforted, . . .
you shall be far from oppression, for you shall not fear."
ISAIAH 54:11, 14 NKJV

In these verses, God speaks to an afflicted person who has suffered from oppressors. Then He describes how she will be rebuilt with precious stones like a beautiful spiritual city (vv. 11–12). The imagery God invokes is strikingly similar to the heavenly Jerusalem in Revelation 21–22, and the similarity is intentional.

Have you suffered abuse in some form? Are you unable to find lasting comfort? Know that God can help you to gain victory over trauma, and He longs for you to experience peace. You can begin to enjoy a foretaste of heaven here and now.

God is able to restore your life and build you up spiritually so that you will be strong and radiant. Allow His Holy Spirit to enter the darkest corners of your memories, wash away the fear, and cleanse you from guilt, anger, and insecurity.

Recovering from abuse can take years, but God can throw aside the curtains in sudden moments of revelation and splash His sunlight into your soul.

Holy Spirit, You know what I have been through. Help me to
have the victory over trauma. I need the peace that only You
can give. Show me how to take the next step toward spiritual
strength and restoration through Your power. Amen.

God Sees Your Plight

The Egyptians abused and battered us,
in a cruel and savage slavery.
DEUTERONOMY 26:6 MSG

Women trapped in abusive relationships and children from dysfunctional families can identify with those words, "abused and battered," yet they describe the desperate plight of God's people in Egypt thirty-five hundred years ago.

The next verse says, "We cried out to GOD. . . . He listened to our voice, he saw our destitution, our trouble, our cruel plight" (Deuteronomy 26:7 MSG). "The Israelites groaned in their slavery and cried out, and their cry for help. . .went up to God" (Exodus 2:23 NIV). God heard them and set them free.

God knows the suffering you have endured, He hears your prayers, and His heart is moved. He will take steps to deliver you from your plight and to comfort you.

He is with you, even in the silence and loneliness, and in your darkest moments when you feel the most damaged and worthless, He looks on you as His own child, of inestimable worth. One day you will meet Him face-to-face and He will wipe all tears from your eyes (Revelation 7:17). In the meantime, He is always with you, comforting you.

God, I know You see me and hear my cries. Deliver me from my suffering. Comfort me. In my darkest moments, shine the light of Your love into my soul. Be with me until I can see You face-to-face because I need You now more than ever. Amen.

Overcoming the Past

*"You make victims of the children and leave
them vulnerable to violence and vice."*
MICAH 2:9 MSG

Frequently, children who are victims of abuse, violence, or neglect grow up insecure and, in later years, look for approval and acceptance in the wrong places. They may seek solace in alcohol or drugs, or search for fulfillment in unhealthy relationships, where they are vulnerable to further violence and vice.

You really have to admire those who had traumatic childhoods and yet are resolving and overcoming their issues to find wholeness and fulfillment. But it is not easy. God offers healing, but it takes a determination to rise above the past, to close the door to anger, and to build a new life in Christ.

"If anyone is in Christ, he is a new creation; old things have passed away; behold, all things have become new" (2 Corinthians 5:17 NKJV). God does a major work in people's heart at salvation, but complete transformation takes a lifetime. "We. . .beholding as in a mirror the glory of the Lord, are being transformed into the same image" (2 Corinthians 3:18 NKJV).

It takes time, but we are being transformed.

---

*Lord, I sometimes struggle with feelings of insecurity. Help
me to come to You with my feelings and anxieties instead of
looking in the wrong places. Continue to transform me daily
into who I am meant to be, made in Your image. Amen.*

Accidents

Occupational Hazards

When you chop wood, there is danger with each stroke of your ax.
ECCLESIASTES 10:9 NLT

When you are injured on the job, you are filled with conflicting thoughts. On the one hand, you know that all occupations have hazards. Soldiers, policemen, and firemen are aware that their jobs are dangerous, but even desk jobs have liabilities.

Still, you may wonder, *Why didn't God protect me?* After all, the Bible promises, "If you. . .make the Most High your dwelling, no harm will overtake you, no disaster will come near your tent. For he will command his angels concerning you to guard you in all your ways" (Psalm 91:9–11 NIV).

Staying close to God definitely guards you from a great deal of misfortune, but the fact is, it won't guarantee you a completely trouble-free existence. The Bible states, "People are born for trouble as readily as sparks fly up from a fire" (Job 5:7 NLT). That's the way life is. We all get sick. We all feel pain. We all have accidents.

But the good news is: "There is wonderful joy ahead, even though you must endure many trials for a little while" (1 Peter 1:6 NLT).

Father, I know I can't avoid all trials because I live in a fallen world. Grant me patience and endurance when they come my way. I know You can take these trials and make me stronger. In the meantime, help me to look for the coming joy. Amen.

Unexpected Injuries

Ahaziah had fallen through the lattice of his
upper room in Samaria and injured himself.

2 KINGS 1:2 NIV

In Bible times, people covered their window openings with thin slats of wood called latticework. One day King Ahaziah was in an upper palace room and leaned heavily against the latticework, causing it to break. He plunged to the courtyard below and was seriously injured (2 Kings 1:2). Because he looked to the false god Baal-Zebub for healing, he died (vv. 16–17).

You may trust in God, but that is not a guarantee that you will never have an accident. The difference is that God constantly works on behalf of His children to bring great good out of tragedies. "All things work together for good to those who love God" (Romans 8:28 NKJV), even accidents.

When you suffer unexpected misfortune, God can see to it that you also experience unexpected good as a result—benefits such as spiritual depth, compassion, and patience.

You might rather do without spiritual benefits and simply enjoy a trouble-free, easy life, but God is seeking to transform you into a better person, and to do so, He often has to bring you through troubled times.

God, I know that this life is full of troubles, but I also know that You can bring good out of any situation. Help me to be patient and discern how You are at work in my life even in the unexpected injuries. Amen.

Unexplained Misfortune

No one can predict misfortune. . . . So men and
women are caught by accidents evil and sudden.
ECCLESIASTES 9:12 MSG

Many Christians believe that nothing happens randomly. They insist that God is in control of events down to the very tiniest details. And since He is able to protect them from all accidents and misfortune, when accidents happen God must have good reasons for allowing them, even if these reasons aren't apparent.

This is true, but to focus on that is to miss the big picture. God is definitely able to micromanage events in believers' lives to bring about His purposes, but it is important to realize that He is focused on the larger issues. The psalmist said of God, "Your thoughts are very deep" (Psalm 92:5 NKJV).

Some people demand, "Why, God?" They insist that God explain His actions. They desire an itemized justification for every injury He allowed. Meanwhile, God's concern is the overall condition of their heart. He is watching whether they will trust Him no matter what.

The fact is, most times in this life you won't understand why God has allowed an accident. So focus on what's most important—loving Him and remaining true to Him through it all.

Father, I don't know why misfortune comes my way, but I know You are
in control. You see the big picture because Your ways are higher than
mine. Help me to trust Your plans even when I don't understand. Amen.

Guarded from Evil

*They will lift you up in their hands, so that you
will not strike your foot against a stone.*

PSALM 91:12 NIV

You may be confused when reading the promises of Psalm 91. Verse 11 (NIV) says that God's angels will "guard you in all your ways." The very next verse promises that they won't even allow you to stub your toe against a stone. However, you know from experience that you and most other believers do suffer injury from time to time, sometimes even serious injuries.

Yet the psalm promises, "No harm will overtake you" (v. 10 NIV). It sounds like you should expect to experience a totally blessed, trouble-free life. So what gives?

The answer is that this is the ideal state, promised when you passionately love God and know Him (v. 14). The opening verse states that these promises are for "whoever dwells in the shelter of the Most High" (v. 1 NIV). You must *constantly* dwell close to God's heart, sheltered by His presence.

Most Christians don't abide that close to God. So although He still protects you, often in direct correlation to how close you are to Him, you will occasionally suffer accidents.

---

*Lord, I know that injuries are part of living in a fallen world,
but You also guard me from many injuries and evils that I never
see. Keep me sheltered in Your presence so that even when I
suffer injury I am still held in Your loving arms. Amen.*

Accidents and Judgment

*"What about the eighteen people who died when the tower in
Siloam fell on them? Were they the worst sinners in Jerusalem?"*
LUKE 13:4 NLT

Many Jews believed there were no such things as "accidents."
Whenever something bad happened to someone, it was considered
God's judgment on sin.

But at a certain level, this rationale breaks down. After all, car-
penters use sharp tools to cut wood and end up with nicks and cuts
fairly frequently (Ecclesiastes 10:9). So only the *biggest* accidents were
considered judgments—but even so, this isn't a cause-and-effect rule
that applies in every case.

Proverbs 26:27 (NKJV) says, "He who rolls a stone will have it
roll back on him," so when eighteen people were killed by collapsing
stones, many Jews were absolutely convinced that those men had
been the worst sinners in the city. But Jesus disputed this.

He said that those men had been no worse than the people
standing around pointing their fingers. They all were sinners, so it
could have happened to any of them (Luke 13:5). Now, God sometimes does judge sin by allowing accidents, but only He knows each
situation, so let's stop judging others.

---

*Holy Spirit, give me a spirit of discernment and grace. The
rain falls on the just and the unjust alike, so help me to leave
judgment in Your capable hands and offer comfort to those
who are suffering from accidents and difficult times. Amen.*

Addiction

Caught in a Vicious Cycle

A man of great wrath shall suffer punishment:
for if thou deliver him, yet thou must do it again.
PROVERBS 19:19 KJV

When you have an addiction, you find yourself compulsively indulging in harmful behavior, even though you know it is destructive. This is true for those prone to anger, but it is also true if your addiction is gambling, overeating, pornography, spending, or alcohol.

Someone may mercifully step in and deliver you from the mess you make of your life and cushion the consequences of your actions, but does that really help? They will just have to do it again next week.

If you have an addiction, Paul's words describe your dilemma: "I obviously need help! . . .I can will it, but I can't do it. I decide to do good, but I don't really do it; I decide not to do bad, but then I do it anyway. . . . Is there no one who can do anything for me? . . . The answer, thank God, is that Jesus Christ can and does" (Romans 7:18–19, 24–25 MSG).

When you finally come to the end of yourself, you are ready for God's solution.

God, I cannot do this alone. Show me my need for You. You are
the only one who can break the cycle and free me from the
chains of addiction and sin. May I place my expectation on
You alone because all other paths lead to failure. Amen.

Lust and Pornography

"I have made a covenant with my eyes;
why then should I look upon a young woman?"
JOB 31:1 NKJV

Many people are addicted to pornography. It starts "harmlessly." They allow their eyes to linger a few seconds on attractive men or women—in person or in the media—while entertaining fleeting thoughts of sexual pleasure. If they make little effort to resist such thoughts, these thoughts become more frequent. Eventually, they begin visiting explicit websites.

They can become addicted to the rushes of excitement, which are, however, followed by guilt and a weakened prayer life. Paul promises, "No temptation has overtaken you except such as is common to man; but God. . .will also make the way of escape, that you may be able to bear it" (1 Corinthians 10:13 NKJV).

Four thousand years ago, Job said, "I have made a covenant with my eyes" (Job 31:1 NKJV). Job knew he had to nip lust in the bud. So he made a firm decision not to allow his eyes to linger on a young woman, not to indulge in even a fleeting lust.

He stopped lust cold—and it kept him from a great deal of trouble.

Lord, my flesh is weak, so keep my eyes locked on You.
I make a covenant with You to not allow my eyes to
linger where they should not and to stop lust in its tracks
before it can gain a foothold in my life. Amen.

Stuck in the Mud

One of the most frustrating things about an addiction is that even though you recognize that it is wreaking havoc in your life, and you make a decision to stop it, it often has such a powerful grip that before you know it, you are at it again.

Although it isn't flattering to envision yourself like a pig rolling in the mud, it may be helpful to look at your addiction in light of this statement. The point of the word picture is that simply attempting to clean up your act on the outside isn't enough. Until you have a change in your basic nature, you will continually return to your addiction after attempts to stop.

That is why you need the life-changing power of the Holy Spirit to take hold of your mind and spirit and bring about lasting change. This usually takes time, and it will certainly take repeated, desperate prayers. You have to really want change, doggedly pursue God, and not give up until He answers your prayers.

Fortunately, God continually gives you another chance, even after you mess up again.

Holy Spirit, search me and cleanse me from the inside out.
I want to change, but I can only do it through Your
power. Strengthen me and help me to persevere through
the process so that I can gain the victory. Amen.

Addicted to Pleasure

You're addicted to thrills? What an empty life!
The pursuit of pleasure is never satisfied.
PROVERBS 21:17 MSG

Addictions come in many forms. Some people are addicted to non-prescription drugs. Many people are addicted to the love hormones, dopamine and norepinephrine, and constantly seek thrills from illicit sexual encounters. They "live for lustful pleasure" (Ephesians 4:19 NLT). Some people's brains release dopamine when they are engaged in extreme sports. They receive a pleasurable reward from high-risk activities and so repeatedly come back for more.

But whether the thrills people pursue are illegal, immoral, or simply insanely dangerous, the Bible says that the constant pursuit of pleasure is never satisfied. A life lived only for selfish pleasure and fulfillment is empty, and it often becomes expensive very quickly. "Those who love pleasure become poor; those who love wine and luxury will never be rich" (Proverbs 21:17 NLT).

People are addicted to things and substances for the rewards they give them. If you want to break free from such addictions and truly enjoy life, you have to find fulfillment in God. "In Your presence is fullness of joy; at Your right hand are pleasures forevermore" (Psalm 16:11 NKJV).

Lord, help me to find pleasure in You and in the blessings
of everyday life. Show me the futility of chasing earthly
pleasures that only lead to disappointment and emptiness.
Fill the empty parts of my soul with Your love. Amen.

Adultery

Adultery Is Destructive

Adultery is a brainless act, soul-destroying, self-destructive.
PROVERBS 6:32 MSG

Adultery truly is a mindless act. It is not that adulterers have no brain; the problem is that they are not listening to it. Against their better judgment, in the face of all they know to be true and right, they ignore their rational minds and allow their bodies to be swept along in a tidal wave of lust. Perhaps this tragedy has happened to you—or to your husband.

God designed the love hormones, dopamine and norepinephrine, to create intense feelings of excitement and romantic passion. He intended a husband and wife to enjoy the pleasures of sex to the full. . . .but He doesn't sanction sex outside of marriage. His Word tells us, "Marriage is honorable among all, and the bed undefiled; but fornicators and adulterers God will judge" (Hebrews 13:4 NKJV).

God will one day judge adulterers, but in the meantime, "a man who commits adultery. . .destroys himself" (Proverbs 6:32 NIV). He destroys integrity, love, trust, his marriage, and sometimes his entire life. If you have gone astray in this way, turn to God and He will have mercy on you.

---

*Holy Spirit, keep my eyes and feet from straying down
a path of destruction. If I do falter, lead me back onto
the straight path. Make me mindful of how my thoughts
and actions affect me and those I love. Amen.*

Adultery in the Heart

*"Anyone who looks at a woman lustfully has
already committed adultery with her in his heart."*
MATTHEW 5:28 NIV

Some of Jesus' listeners were astonished when He informed them that a man who looks at a woman with sexual lust and fantasizes about having sex with her has already committed adultery with her in his heart. But that is precisely what he is doing. Jesus didn't say the man had literally committed adultery. He said the man had done it "in his heart."

The Lord also wasn't talking about a passing thought—something most people experience—which they immediately resist. Some people have been needlessly condemned over this. Jesus was talking about focusing on someone with intense desire.

Most people, when they fantasize about having an adulterous affair, purposefully fill their thoughts with lurid mental images. This is what God was warning against when He said, "You shall not covet your neighbor's wife" (Deuteronomy 5:21 NIV). To "covet" means to earnestly, persistently desire, to set one's heart on something.

Eventually this leads to thoughts of how to actually *have* that person, not merely imagine it. That is why it is vital to not even start down that path.

God, may I keep my eyes and my imagination pure.
Help me to guard my heart. Give me strength to block
temptation from gaining a foothold in my mind before it
can take control of my actions and my life. Amen.

Obsessed with Adultery

They're obsessed with adultery, compulsive in sin,
seducing every vulnerable soul they come upon.

2 PETER 2:14 MSG

Many men and women are addicted to adultery. It gives them a rush. They are constantly on the lookout for dissatisfied married people who can be flattered and enticed to indulge in an illicit affair. Many men "creep into households and make captives of gullible women loaded down with sins, led away by various lusts" (2 Timothy 3:6 NKJV).

Of course, some women are the initiators. Like Potiphar's wife, they are continuously looking for new bed partners (Genesis 39:7–12). The Bible warns, "Don't. . .be taken in by her bedroom eyes" (Proverbs 6:25 MSG). And though "the lips of the adulterous woman drip honey" (Proverbs 5:3 NIV), they lead to death.

God knows that even if you are married, you will still find other members of the opposite sex attractive, and at times your hormones will fill you with powerful waves of desire. But don't give in to them, or the day will come when you deeply regret it. Once you have betrayed your husband or wife, it can take a long time and many prayers and tears to rebuild his or her trust.

Holy Spirit, give me the discernment to identify those who would try to entice me or manipulate me into an illicit affair. Give me the strength to avoid temptation or, like Joseph with Potiphar's wife, to run away from compromising situations. Amen.

Commonsense Commandment

"You must not commit adultery."
EXODUS 20:14 NLT

Five short words, but they serve to safeguard you from a very destructive sin. God knew that most people would—at some point or another—be tempted to commit adultery, so He put up a billboard commanding you not to do it.

Remember, "No temptation has overtaken you except what is *common* to mankind" (1 Corinthians 10:13 NIV, emphasis added).

Sexual attraction is a powerful force, and God designed it to help bond husbands and wives together. But even believers, if they are not careful, can be overcome by the siren call of extramarital sex. That is why you must internalize God's command and take steps to keep yourself safe.

You can't keep from noticing that someone is sexually attractive—especially if they have gone to great pains to make themselves look that way—but you can keep your eyes from sneaking back for a second and third glance.

If you find your imagination constantly excited by someone else's husband or wife, persistently resist such thoughts. Take definite steps to make sure that you don't ever end up alone with that person. Do this and God will keep you from falling.

Lord, help me to keep Your Word close to my heart and my focus on You so that I can resist temptation and avoid compromising situations. Only with Your help and strength can I follow Your commandments. Only You can keep me from falling. Amen.

Heating Up Ovens

"They are all adulterers. Like an oven heated by a baker. . . . They are all hot, like an oven."
HOSEA 7:4, 7 NKJV

Feelings of sexual desire can be very powerful. Such passion is entirely appropriate with your husband or wife, but inappropriate outside marriage.

Hosea compared the adulterers of Israel to "an oven heated by a baker," where the baker added fuel to the barely burning coals in the oven. Hosea 7:4 (NKJV) adds, "He ceases stirring the fire after kneading the dough." But up until that time the baker had worked to *stir up* a blazing fire.

Just so, people who commit adultery usually feed the flames of desire with sexual images. Adultery is often a deliberate, premeditated act. One good way to avoid this is to get rid of any fuel so you can't feed the fire. This means ridding your home of pornography and refusing to view it on the Internet. Doing these things will greatly reduce the problem.

In addition, remember the Bible's advice: "It is better to marry than to burn with passion" (1 Corinthians 7:9 NKJV). And if you are already married, be satisfied with that (Proverbs 5:18–20).

Father, search my heart and life; show me anything that is fuel to a dangerous flame. Help me to remove it from my life. Strengthen my resolve to follow Your Word and live a life that is honorable and brings You glory. Amen.

Alcohol Abuse

Overcoming Alcoholism

*Who has needless bruises? Who has bloodshot
eyes? Those who linger over wine.*
PROVERBS 23:29–30 NIV

If you have a problem with alcohol, you don't need to be told that it is wrong. You already know that. You know that it is wasting your hard-earned cash, that it is wrecking your marriage, and that it leaves you filled with remorse and despair. And then there are those totally needless bruises. The question is, what are you going to do about it?

Until you are desperate enough to surrender your life to God, there is not a whole lot you can do. You have already tried to stop yourself but have repeatedly fallen off the wagon.

Here is where the biblical principles behind Alcoholics Anonymous can help: you must honestly admit your sins, confess your faults to someone else, and trust God for the power to change. There is more to it, but these are an excellent start.

As a Christian, you know that the higher power is Jesus, the Son of God. He said, "Apart from me you can do nothing" (John 15:5 NIV). And Paul wrote, "I can do everything through Christ, who gives me strength" (Philippians 4:13 NLT).

---

*Lord, I need help. I cannot do this in my own strength.
I surrender my will to You. Cleanse me and make me a new
creature. Help me to break free of the chains of addiction
and sin through the power of the Holy Spirit. Amen.*

Downsides of Alcohol

Wine produces mockers; alcohol leads to brawls.
Those led astray by drink cannot be wise.

PROVERBS 20:1 NLT

Alcohol removes inhibitions and sets people's base natures loose. A person under the influence of drinking is often loud and confrontational. Some people become happy and make jokes or boast; others become angry and mock or argue. The latter often leads to drunken fights.

"Those led astray by drink cannot be wise." Have you ever seen an inebriated man giving someone advice? Though he may think he is sharing words of profound wisdom, to the sober listener it is utter foolishness.

The only time you can be truly wise is when you are sober. That is when it pays to take a long, hard look at the benefits and downsides of drinking. Alcohol does offer a temporary escape from trouble. This is why many people turn to it to unwind and forget, or to have a "good time." Unfortunately, it also causes many problems, problems that are not temporary.

If you struggle with alcohol, it is wise to make yourself accountable to others who understand your struggle. Listen to their advice and then act on it day by day.

God, give me wise friends who will give good support and advice as well as hold me accountable when I struggle. True wisdom comes from following Your Word and doing Your commands. Grant me wisdom and willpower when I am tempted. Amen.

Boasting about Drinking

What sorrow for those who are heroes at drinking wine
and boast about all the alcohol they can hold.

ISAIAH 5:22 NLT

Sometimes what you thought was a strength, something to be proud of, was actually a weakness. The fact that you once boasted about your drinking was a sure sign that you had set yourself up for grief. If you now have sobriety, you can look back and shake your head in disbelief at such a mindset.

If you are still struggling to gain mastery over the bottle, you may already be aware that boasting about how much liquor you can hold is stupid. But knowing that isn't enough. You can still be fooled by thinking, *But one drink can't hurt—after all, it takes a lot for me to get drunk*. But one glass leads to many more.

If you have any pride left at all about drinking, or if you are still amused by your antics when intoxicated, you are not ready to abandon alcohol and put your life back together. As cliché as this sounds, you may actually have to hit rock bottom before you are ready for God's solution.

Father, search my heart and show me if there is any
pride in me regarding this area. Help me to see the truth,
even if I have to hit rock bottom, because I know You
will be there to help me when I call on Your name. Amen.

Getting Flaming Drunk

What sorrow for those who. . .spend long evenings
drinking wine to make themselves flaming drunk.
ISAIAH 5:11 NLT

Those who have a full-blown case of alcoholism have little control over their addiction. However, not all people have an advanced case of this addiction, particularly at the beginning. Often, when they are first giving in to drink, they have a choice in the matter.

That is why the Bible warns you not to binge drink just to experience what it is like to be completely drunk. Not only are you starting down a very slippery slope that could become a lifelong habit of destruction, but think of the damage you can cause in just one night!

The young are especially tempted to prove how much alcohol they can hold or just how much of a spectacle they are willing to make of themselves. Many see out-of-control drunkenness as a rite of passage or a way to earn respect or acceptance. What sorrow they earn instead!

Why wait until things get so bad that alcohol has become your master and you must fight a protracted battle to take back your life? It is better to stop before you even start.

Lord, give me the wisdom and strength to avoid the
slippery path of allowing alcohol to have free rein in my
life. Let me learn from others' mistakes, and give me the
strength to say no when temptation finds me. Amen.

Anger

Controlling Your Temper

Do not hasten in your spirit to be angry,
for anger rests in the bosom of fools.
ECCLESIASTES 7:9 NKJV

The New International Version says it this way: "Do not be quickly provoked in your spirit." In other words, exercise self-control and don't allow yourself to be easily provoked. Whether you believe that you can do it or not, God expects you to be able to control your temper.

James writes, "Let every man be. . .slow to wrath" (James 1:19 NKJV), and you might have to bite down on your tongue to avoid giving in to it.

The Bible also says, "A fool's wrath is known at once. . . . A fool rages. . . . A quick-tempered man acts foolishly" (Proverbs 12:16; 14:16, 17 NKJV). Remind yourself: if you continue to lose your temper easily, you are behaving like a fool—and the Bible gives clear warnings about fools: "The mouth of the foolish is near destruction. . . . A fool lays open his folly. . . . The foolishness of a man twists his way. . . . A fool vents all his feelings" (Proverbs 10:14; 13:16; 19:3; 29:11 NKJV).

Exercising self-control is well worth it.

Holy Spirit, help me to control my tongue and be aware
of how the enemy is trying to use me for his own purposes.
Show me when my temper is getting the better of me
so that it doesn't make me into a fool. Amen.

Be Slow to Anger

Let every man be swift to hear, slow to speak, slow to wrath.
JAMES 1:19 KJV

Many people are easygoing. They aren't easily riled. Other people have a short fuse and struggle with anger issues most of their lives. They know they should simply let things go, but at the slightest provocation, their temper flares up. Is there no solution?

There may not be an easy solution, but there is a solution. James tells us, "Let every man be. . .slow to wrath" (James 1:19 KJV). He says *every* man. This tells us that with God's help, we all can gain control of our tempers. No exceptions.

However, we often first need to renounce our pride. Some people actually boast, "Whoa! You should see me when I get mad!" The Bible addresses pride-motivated statements, saying, "All such boasting is evil" (James 4:16 NKJV).

Second, we must cry out to God for help. Third, we need to make a constant effort to have patience. Giving others the benefit of the doubt and refusing to jump to conclusions can defuse many arguments and provocations before they begin.

Lord, I know I need to work on this area of my life. Help me to admit my pride and ask for Your strength and guidance in my communications with others. Help me to persevere so that I can be a peacemaker in an angry world. Amen.

Hot Tempers and Conflict

An angry person stirs up conflict, and a
hot-tempered person commits many sins.
PROVERBS 29:22 NIV

Whether you are an angry person or are close to an angry person, you know how easily someone with a temper can be set off. At the slightest provocation, voices are raised, accusations are made, and the fight is on. Lighting an angry person's fuse is easy, and once lit, the person explodes.

Pride and a brooding sense of injustice are often at the root. Angry people are quick to imagine that someone has insulted them and to take offense. They constantly stir up fights and, in the process, commit many sins.

Try this: *pray* for those who anger you, commit them into God's hands, ask Him to bless them richly, and pray that He will give you love, empathy, and understanding for them. "The LORD turned the captivity of Job, when he prayed for his friends" (Job 42:10 KJV).

When you earnestly pray for others' good, you more easily forgive and overlook their faults. And if you are overlooking their faults, you won't be prone to be angry with them.

Father, I don't want to live my life in anger and frustration.
I want to live it in peace with You, myself, and others, so let
me see others through Your eyes of love and compassion—
the same love and compassion you showed to me. Amen.

Quick-Tempered Folly

If you are plagued by a quick temper, it might seem frustrating to hear that the solution is to have lots of patience—as if there were a choice in the matter! Your anger might appear to be like a tidal wave that rises up in an instant without warning, at the slightest provocation. It might seem as if you have no control over it.

The truth is, however, that you can eventually master it if you are determined to do so. It will take time and concentrated effort, and it may even take attending a few anger management courses. But the more you understand why you react the way you do and recognize your trigger points, the more control you will have.

Another strategy for reining in your temper is to make a concerted effort to understand others as well. If you begin to understand what motivates them, you are less likely to take offense. And if you determine to be patient with people and to love them with God's love, you can actually begin to govern your anger.

Lord, I want to be patient, but sometimes I let the world get the better of me. Show me ways I can avoid losing my temper. Give me insight into what others are going through so that I can minister to them with patience and understanding. Amen.

Controlling Your Temper

Sensible people control their temper;
they earn respect by overlooking wrongs.
PROVERBS 19:11 NLT

Even smart people can have a quick temper. However, they recognize that their anger is a problem, so they take steps to control it. They don't want to hurt others or make a bad situation worse.

If you have anger issues, there are things you can do. First, the Bible says to overlook wrongs. Solomon said, "Do not pay attention to every word people say" (Ecclesiastes 7:21 NIV) but remind yourself that you too say things you shouldn't. If you can, let it pass.

Second, make up your mind ahead of time that when provoked, you won't respond with an angry outburst.

Third, don't answer quickly, but take time to pray and think through a calm response.

Fourth, when you express yourself, avoid making blanket accusations such as, "You always. . ." Instead, explain how the offender's actions or words make you feel.

Fifth, instead of focusing on what made you angry, suggest solutions to the problem.

Sixth, when really angry, take some time out to exercise.

Seventh, pray and meditate on peaceful subjects before reengaging with the person who offended you.

God, sometimes I struggle with my temper. I want to be sensible
and wise, but I need You to teach me better ways to solve problems
by dealing with provocation before it becomes an issue. Amen.

Anxiety

Avoiding Anxiety

So what do people get. . .for all their hard work
and anxiety?. . . At night their minds cannot rest.
ECCLESIASTES 2:22–23 NLT

A habit of worry leads to an anxious mind. Anxiety is a decision not to trust God, but to instead scramble around trying to solve your own problems. You may find yourself slipping so naturally into a worried attitude that it doesn't even seem like a conscious decision. But it is.

What starts off as a small worry quickly grows into a frenzied effort to work things out. But it is all a waste of time.

The first step to overcoming anxiety is to realize that worrying is a surefire way to sabotage success. Being anxious all day is very tiring, yet it robs you of sleep at night. And knowing that you won't be able to do your best if you are sleep deprived gives you something else to worry about.

The best way to fight anxiety is to continually look to the Lord, constantly quote Bible promises to yourself, and refuse to give an inch to worry. It will be hard at first, but don't worry: it gets easier as time goes on.

Father, help me to trust You instead of striving to fix things on my own. When anxiety threatens to overcome me and take away my peace, bring scriptures to my memory that remind me of Your love and power so that I can hand the situation over to You. Amen.

Wearing Yourself Out

*It is useless for you to work so hard from early
morning until late at night, anxiously working for
food to eat; for God gives rest to his loved ones.*
PSALM 127:2 NLT

Many people think that worry is a trifling thing, something that frays the outer edges of their minds but really isn't a problem. But anxiety can suck the very life out of you. If you fear that setbacks are inevitable and constantly fret that your finances aren't sufficient, you will work harder to compensate for the lack. And if you work when you should be resting, you will wear yourself out.

The thing is, there may not even be a lack on your horizon. You just worry that there will be, so you give yourself stomach ulcers and overwork for nothing. Now, it is prudent to make sure that you have sufficient finances, but anxiety is beyond prudent. It's a failure to believe that God cares for you.

David wrote, "In the multitude of my anxieties within me, Your comforts delight my soul" (Psalm 94:19 NKJV). David did what he could, but after that he trusted the Lord and allowed God to comfort him.

---

*Father, help me to do my best and trust You with the rest.
Bring to my mind all the ways You have provided for
me in the past. Give me the peace only You can give so
that I can rest knowing You are in control. Amen.*

Don't Be Anxious

*Do not be anxious about anything, but in every
situation. . .present your requests to God.*
PHILIPPIANS 4:6 NIV

Say you are out shopping and you suddenly realize you have lost
your keys or your cell phone. You are hit with panic, and as time
crawls on, you get a sinking feeling of how bad this situation is. The
normal tendency is to let wave after wave of anxiety roll over you.

But the Bible says, "Do not be anxious about *anything*, but in
every situation. . .present your requests to God" (Philippians 4:6 NIV,
emphasis added). No exceptions. So that is what you should do: ask
God to do a miracle and help you locate it or to have some honest
person find it and turn it in.

It doesn't have to be an emergency either. It could simply be a
situation that is bad and slowly getting worse, and over which you
have little control. Rather than letting it suck the life out of you, you
need to be able to turn it over to God.

You aren't guaranteed that God will reunite you with your missing
items, but He can at least limit the damage that their loss may cause.

---

*Holy Spirit, when anxieties arise in me, help me to stop and
bring them to You. Help me to make it a habit of coming to You
first instead of worrying about situations. I need the peace that
passes understanding and that only comes from You. Amen.*

Bankruptcy

When Everything Is Gone

"My husband is dead, and. . .now his creditor is coming to take my two boys as his slaves."

2 Kings 4:1 niv

More than a hundred prophets followed Elisha around to learn from him. One of them had a wife and two young boys. They had a small mud-brick house but little else. The prophet apparently became sick and unable to work, so he was forced to borrow money to buy food.

He probably hoped to recover and get back to work, but instead he grew steadily worse and died. The creditor demanded repayment, but since the widow had absolutely nothing, he came to enslave her two sons and work them to pay the debt. But Elisha prayed, and God did a miracle to provide the money she needed.

Bankruptcy wasn't really an option in Old Testament times. People had to pay one way or another. We today can be thankful. Even though bankruptcy is a difficult and humiliating ordeal, and recovery can take years, things aren't as harsh as they were in Elisha's day.

If you have had to declare bankruptcy, thank God for seeing you through it.

Father, You know my situation, and only You know the best course of action. Give me wisdom and humility. I know You will walk with me through this season, even though sometimes it doesn't feel like it, because You said You will never leave me nor forsake me. Amen.

Riches to Rags

"The Almighty has made life very bitter for me. I went
away full, but the LORD has brought me home empty."

RUTH 1:20–21 NLT

During a long drought in Israel, Naomi and her husband, Elimelech, became desperate for food. When their money ran out, they had to move to Moab in search of employment.

Today both societies and individuals experience financial droughts. You may have gone through a prolonged period of unemployment that drained your savings and forced you to declare bankruptcy.

When this happened, you may have wondered why God decided to make your life bitter. Usually, however, when people go bankrupt, it is not God's doing. Often they are reaping the results of their own financial mismanagement. However, sometimes an entire society goes through a recession. Then many innocent people suffer.

Don't become bitter against God. Trust that He will see you through the crisis. In the meantime, practice what Paul wrote: "I have learned how to be content with whatever I have. I know how to live on almost nothing or with everything" (Philippians 4:11–12 NLT).

Lord, help me to be content no matter what situation I am
in by helping me keep my focus on You. Help me to trust
that You will work it all out for my good and Your glory
because I know You want the best for me. Amen.

Experiencing Financial Ruin

Let the creditor seize all that he has,
and let strangers plunder his labor.
PSALM 109:11 NKJV

Bankruptcy in Bible times was an even more traumatic experience than it is today. When a wicked man was accusing him falsely and fighting against him without just cause, David prayed, "Let the creditor seize all that he has."

This was one of the most devastating things David could have wished on an enemy. A creditor would literally seize *all* that a person had—going so far as to press him and his family into slavery to work off their debt. At least today, if you are forced into bankruptcy, the trustees are supposed to see to it that you are left with enough to live on.

In today's troubled economy, it is not only the wicked and the reckless who experience bankruptcy. Yes, often people end up there due to overspending or financial decisions that, in hindsight, weren't the wisest—but sometimes the innocent are driven into financial ruin by circumstances beyond their control.

God is able to rescue you from the deepest pit you find yourself in and establish your feet on solid ground again.

God, You know my heart and my situation. Only You can rescue me. I know that You have my best interests at heart. Help me to accept Your will even if it is not the answer I hoped for. Amen.

Hope after Bankruptcy

I will restore to you the years that the locust hath eaten.
JOEL 2:25 KJV

Locusts are a type of winged grasshopper that live, among other places, in the deserts of North Africa. Under certain conditions, they begin to breed abundantly and then migrate. In Bible times, they descended on Israel in swarms of eighty billion strong.

They caused unimaginable damage, devouring grain crops and vineyards, and even stripping the leaves off trees. Everyone suffered loss and saw the hard work of years wiped out. God said that He sent locusts as punishment but promised that if His people repented, "I will forgive their sin and will heal their land" (2 Chronicles 7:14 NIV).

There is hope of similar healing after bankruptcy. God can likewise restore to you the many years of loss that such an event has wiped out. It will take time, but bankruptcy, hard as it may be, can teach you valuable lessons and a sense of priorities that will serve you well in the future.

If you are going through bankruptcy or recovering from one, take hope. God is in the business of helping people get back on their feet after heavy losses.

God, it feels like the locusts are swarming around me. You know my heart and my financial situation. Help me to trust You more and give me Your peace during this time of trial because my only hope is in You. Amen.

Betrayal

When Friends Betray You

My best friend, the one I trusted completely,
the one who shared my food, has turned against me.
PSALM 41:9 NLT

Betrayal hurts, especially when the person who betrayed you was a close friend, someone you shared your most intimate thoughts with. You trusted him. Then you learned that he went about as a gossip, either carelessly or maliciously telling your deepest secrets.

We all have experienced betrayal in one form or another. Perhaps you have betrayed someone. Even if you didn't intentionally cross her, she feels that you did, or that you went back on your word, let her down, or told others things she had confided to you.

It is difficult to make amends if the one you betrayed no longer wishes to speak to you and refuses to trust you again. Since you know how that feels, make sure never to put someone else through the wringer for a similar blunder.

Discern between a malicious betrayal (by someone you must avoid confiding in again) and a friend who made an honest mistake (but who deserves another chance, and whom you can still trust). Forgive everyone, but use wisdom in restoring people to your confidence.

Holy Spirit, my friend has turned against me. Give me
discernment in knowing the heart of the person who has
betrayed me, and give me the wisdom to know how to handle
the situation in a godly manner that will honor You. Amen.

Untrustworthy Gossips

A gadabout gossip can't be trusted with a secret.
PROVERBS 11:13 MSG

Sometimes you let down your guard and tell another person confidential things you probably shouldn't. He is your friend. You trust him. What could go wrong? But misunderstandings happen, and when they do, friends get offended. And then a friend, who now has a grudge against you, is in possession of information that could cause you embarrassment or damage.

Or maybe there was no misunderstanding. Maybe a friend simply wasn't trustworthy to begin with because she just couldn't resist the temptation to share some juicy gossip.

Sometimes you are blindsided by betrayal. But often you set yourself up for pain by trusting someone against your better judgment. This is why David wrote, "I will hold my tongue when the ungodly are around me" (Psalm 39:1 NLT). And at times you need to refrain from telling *anyone*. "Don't trust your neighbor, don't confide in your friend" (Micah 7:5 MSG).

Of course, you need to be able to share your heart with friends, and fortunately there *are* good, trustworthy people. Know who can be trusted and stick to confiding in them.

Holy Spirit, give me discernment so that I can know who to trust and who not to trust. Help me to know when to speak and when to hold my tongue. I want to find people I can confide in, but I need Your guidance. Amen.

A Legacy of Abuse

Those who betray their own friends leave
a legacy of abuse to their children.
JOB 17:5 MSG

Some people are users. They feel that other people exist for their benefit, perhaps to borrow money from (with no intention of repaying) or to use for momentary sexual gratification and then toss aside. They befriend people, intending to use them and betray their trust.

If you have suffered at the hands of such people, learn to recognize them and avoid being taken in. Learn to say no to their sob stories, and refuse to let them use you again.

"They are like shameless shepherds who care only for themselves. They are like clouds blowing over the land without giving any rain. . . . They are like wild waves of the sea, churning up the foam of their shameful deeds" (Jude 1:12–13 NLT).

While they are hurting others, they are living a self-destructive lifestyle, and they themselves will eventually suffer most. Such lack of concern and loyalty eventually comes back to haunt them, wreaking havoc in their own lives and in the lives of their children, who are influenced by their lack of morals.

Lord, help me to identify those who would use and betray me,
but also help me to be a witness to them and minister to the people
they betray and their families who suffer from their behavior. Give
me wisdom and guidance along with love and compassion. Amen.

Responding to Betrayal

*"Then many will be offended, will betray
one another, and will hate one another."*

MATTHEW 24:10 NKJV

Chances are, someone whom you trusted has ended up betraying you. In a society dominated by self-centered attitudes, it is not surprising to see loyalties and friendships casually cast aside. It is a sign of the times, the steady deterioration of a once-moral society.

Jesus warned that in the last days many people would abandon their faith and would betray their former fellow believers. But how are you supposed to respond in such cases—and how should you react when someone betrays you for any reason?

Jesus gave the answer when He said, "Love your enemies, do good to those who hate you, bless those who curse you, and pray for those who spitefully use you" (Luke 6:27–28 NKJV). Yes, He expects you to forgive someone who has betrayed you, even if you can no longer trust that person and would no longer choose her or him as a confidant and friend.

It is important for your own sake that you forgive them. That way you keep your life free from bitterness and you are not carrying hatred around inside you.

---

*Father, when betrayal comes, help me to forgive and love those
who have hurt me just as You have loved and forgiven me when
I have sinned against You. Please give me wisdom in knowing
how to deal with future interactions in a godly manner. Amen.*

Challenges
Eyes on God

*"O our God, will You not judge them? For we have no power. . . ;
nor do we know what to do, but our eyes are upon You."*
2 CHRONICLES 20:12 NKJV

Christians are no strangers to problems. Sometimes it may seem that your life is *filled* with challenges, setbacks, and obstacles. At such times, you can only look to God and cry out, "Do not withhold Your tender mercies from me, O LORD. . . . For innumerable evils have surrounded me" (Psalm 40:11–12 NKJV).

These challenges could be opposition in the workplace, financial problems, a serious long-term illness, or malicious people who seek to ruin your reputation.

In King Jehoshaphat's day, three enemy nations invaded Judah. They vastly outnumbered the Jews. Jehoshaphat and his people were overwhelmed. They had no idea what to do because there was nothing they could do. So they looked to God and cried out to Him.

God did a miracle to deliver them, and He can do the same for you today. He promises in His Word, "You will seek me and find me when you seek me with all your heart" (Jeremiah 29:13 NIV).

---

*God, when I face challenges, remind me to seek You
first because I can do nothing without You. Only You
can handle the situation. Help me because I don't
know what to do. You are my only hope. Amen.*

Relief from Attacks

Be merciful to me, O God, for man would
swallow me up; fighting all day he oppresses me.
PSALM 56:1 NKJV

Sometimes opponents are relentless in their attacks. They get it into their heads that they should cause you grief and therefore try everything they can think of to oppose you. They keep at it day after day. That is when you desperately need to pray for God to protect you.

Malicious busybodies can cause you a great deal of pain when they take it on themselves to ruin your reputation or get others to shun you. And when they are popular or influential, their persecution amounts to oppression. They may be either open or discreet about their attacks, but the end result is the same.

David experienced this kind of oppression. Even though he was the king of Israel, he had many powerful foes whose tongues secretly worked like razors against him (Psalm 52:2). Read what he wrote in the Psalms and you will draw great comfort from it.

While you can and should speak up to defend your reputation and set the record straight, know that your best defense is prayer. God will be a shield to you and protect you.

Lord, You know me and those who are seeking to destroy my
reputation. For the sake of Your name, be merciful to me and
bring the truth to light. Show me when to speak and when to
be silent, and help me to wait on You to defend me. Amen.

But for God's Help

If you think about it, you can probably remember times when you
came a hairbreadth away from disaster but were spared. This includes
traffic collisions or financial calamity or times when vindictive people
made you their target. These close brushes happen all too often.

You may wonder why God allows such a barrage of challenges.
But it is the world and merciless enemies, not God, that mount constant attrition against you. God steps in as your wall of protection,
preventing the ongoing attacks from sweeping you away.

Still, you may become weary of all this and worry that one day
God will fail to be there for you. David wavered at one point. He had
been pursued for years by King Saul's armies and finally thought,
"Someday Saul is going to get me" (1 Samuel 27:1 NLT).

But it never happened. So don't give up before the bell rings.
God has your back. Stay faithful, and He won't allow your enemies
to swallow you up.

---

*Father, I know You are for me and none can come against me
unless You allow it. So, help me to trust You and believe that
You have my best interests at heart. Give me peace and the
patience to wait on You to work in my situation. Amen.*

Feeling Overwhelmed

We were crushed and overwhelmed beyond our ability to
endure, and we thought we would never live through it.

2 CORINTHIANS 1:8 NLT

Paul and his fellow workers went through really tough times. At one point, he candidly stated, "We were crushed and overwhelmed beyond our ability to endure." But you notice that he did endure, as did his companions. But had the situation continued, they wouldn't have.

God sometimes allows you to go through intolerable circumstances that, if they lasted much longer, would finish you. So Paul wasn't exaggerating when he thought he might not make it. He actually wouldn't have.

Some people harbor a niggling suspicion that God is cruel for allowing believers to go through such severe suffering and testing. But Paul put things in perspective when he said in that same epistle, "For our light affliction, which is but for a moment, is working for us a far more exceeding and eternal weight of glory" (2 Corinthians 4:17 NKJV).

What at the moment is an unendurable crushing will be, in hindsight, "light affliction." You have to see the troubles of this life in the light of heaven to arrive at that conclusion.

Lord, when circumstances feel like they are crushing me,
be near me and comfort me. Help me to see the bigger picture,
but when I don't, help me to trust that I will understand
one day, even if it is not this side of heaven. Amen.

Surviving Oppression

"Many a time they have afflicted me from my youth;
yet they have not prevailed against me."

PSALM 129:2 NKJV

Some people have been picked on for as long as they can remember. Ever since they were little, people bullied them because of some disability—or over their weight or some other physical feature. This was hard to bear, but they refused to succumb, no matter how discouraged they became.

"Those were the hard times! Kicked around in public, targets of every kind of abuse. . . . Nothing they did bothered you, nothing set you back" (Hebrews 10:32–34 MSG). Perhaps you suffered this way, and the memories of it often do bother you. Some people become introverted and depressed over such treatment and even develop suicidal tendencies.

But you survived and became more empathetic and compassionate toward others who also suffered from bullies. Perhaps, though you wouldn't care to repeat the experience, it even made you stronger.

Christian life is often similar. Paul says, "It has been granted to you on behalf of Christ not only to believe in him, but also to suffer for him" (Philippians 1:29 NIV).

God, help me to forgive those who have oppressed me and to use
the strength and compassion that I have gained from the experience
to be an advocate for others who are oppressed. Help me to leave
vengeance in Your hands and move forward with my life. Amen.

Life Is Often Difficult

*"We must go through many hardships
to enter the kingdom of God."*

Acts 14:22 NIV

Sometimes God calls you to bear the almost unbearable. You might be asked to endure prolonged financial insecurity, a debilitating illness, or family turmoil.

You may ask God why, but even more worrying, you ask yourself if God has abandoned you. But take heart in what one Hebrew psalmist declared: "You, who have shown me great and severe troubles, shall revive me again" (Psalm 71:20 NKJV).

If God plans on delivering you and has "plans to give you hope and a future" (Jeremiah 29:11 NIV), you may ask why He lets you experience such trouble in the first place. Well, He knows that as painful as these testings can be, good can come from them. He told the Jews: "I have refined you, but not as silver is refined. Rather, I have refined you in the furnace of suffering" (Isaiah 48:10 NLT).

Jesus said, "Narrow is the gate and difficult is the way which leads to life" (Matthew 7:14 NKJV). He promised that His followers would experience hardships. It's the price you must pay to walk as Jesus walked.

---

*Jesus, I know You suffered greatly so that I might enjoy
eternal salvation and a relationship with You. Help me
to endure suffering here, knowing that it is refining
and shaping me to be more like You. Amen.*

Chronic Illness

Sick for Years

She had suffered a great deal from many doctors, and. . .spent everything she had to pay them, but she had gotten no better.
MARK 5:26 NLT

There once was a woman who had a blood flow like a continual period. She had suffered for years, and despite seeking out the best physicians and spending all her savings on them, her suffering continued unabated.

Then she heard that Jesus, a holy man and healer, was in the city. But she couldn't ask Him to place His hands on her to heal her, for her condition made her ritually impure. Anyone who touched her would become "unclean." That is why she approached Him from behind and secretly touched His robe to tap into His power. And she was healed.

Many people today have chronic illnesses as well. Like this woman, they suffer silently and in shame, convinced that their condition is a judgment from God. But the Lord looks down with eyes of love. "Jesus. . .had compassion on them and healed their sick" (Matthew 14:14 NIV).

Whether you find healing through physicians or the great physician, know that God loves you.

Lord, I know that even if I am not healed this side of heaven, I will one day have a glorified body that is free from all illness. In the meantime, strengthen me so that I may endure through Your grace and mercy. Amen.

Sick a Long Time

*One of the men lying there had
been sick for thirty-eight years.*

JOHN 5:5 NLT

When you read the Gospels and see how often Jesus healed people, you get an idea of how many people were sick, had disabilities, or were suffering from infirmities. A huge percentage of society was sick, and some people had suffered chronic illnesses most of their lives. Think of the man at the pool of Siloam. He had been bedridden for thirty-eight years.

The world's population is much greater today, and the number of sick people is also much greater. Chances are good that you know several people who are suffering long-term illnesses or disabilities. The fact is, even churches that believe in healing have members who suffer on an ongoing basis.

Thank God when He heals people. And thank God for modern medicine that can also alleviate much suffering. But sometimes people suffer for years without a great deal of relief.

You really have to admire some people for how they manage to cope with limited health. They have learned both patience and humility. And while they long to be healed, they maintain a positive attitude through their condition.

---

*Thank You, God, for Your healing power and for advances
in modern medicine. I know You are able to heal me if it's
in Your will; however, I thank You for being with me even
if healing doesn't come this side of heaven. Amen.*

Incurable, Evil Diseases

*"An evil disease," they say, "clings to him. And now
that he lies down, he will rise up no more."*
PSALM 41:8 NKJV

God warned the Israelites that if they persistently disobeyed Him, He would allow them to be afflicted with the evil diseases they had known in Egypt. "The LORD will afflict you with the boils of Egypt and with tumors, festering sores and the itch, from which you cannot be cured" (Deuteronomy 28:27 NIV).

Fast-forward to modern times: not only is it discouraging to have an illness you can't be cured of, but you are also left wondering what sin you committed. Now, some diseases are brought on by sin, and many are caused by unhealthy lifestyle choices, so you may be at fault—but not necessarily.

Even if so, the good news is that God can heal incurable, "evil" diseases. Although David's enemies were convinced that God was judging him and he was done for, David declared, "The LORD will strengthen him on his bed of illness; You will sustain him on his sickbed" (Psalm 41:3 NKJV). And God *did* heal him.

Chronic illnesses don't necessarily have to be forever.

---

*God, You know my health issues. If unconfessed sin or unhealthy
choices are at the root of my illness, show me how to change
for the better. If not, comfort me in my time of distress. I
know You have the power to heal me, but I trust You to know
what is best for me even if it is not Your will. Amen.*

Enduring Illness

My wound is incurable! Yet I said to myself,
"This is my sickness, and I must endure it."
JEREMIAH 10:19 NIV

Jeremiah warned his nation that if they didn't repent of their idolatry, God would send the Babylonians to conquer them. The Lord would give them many opportunities to repent, but He knew that they wouldn't, so their doom was sure. Jeremiah spoke for the nation, saying, "My wound is incurable!" He also knew that their judgment was just, so he said, "This is my sickness, and I must endure it."

Sometimes you will feel the same way if you have a chronic illness. God isn't necessarily judging you for some sin, however. You may simply be sick because you live in a fallen world and your physical body is susceptible to disease.

Certainly God can heal, and you do well to claim His promises and pray for a miracle. And if you have the faith and it is God's will, He will heal you. No disease is incurable to Him.

But if God *doesn't* heal you, you must have the fortitude to say, "This is my sickness, and I must endure it."

Father, I believe You can heal me if You choose, but if it is not Your will, then give me strength and perseverance to carry on Your plan for my life and to endure this sickness in a way that glorifies You. Amen.

Severe Illnesses

Though his disease was severe, . . .he did not seek
help from the Lord, but only from the physicians.
2 CHRONICLES 16:12 NIV

Doctors can now cure "incurable" diseases. For example, about four hundred million people died from the Black Death in the 1300s. The mortality rate in some places was 95 percent. Cases of plague occasionally occur today, but the victims usually recover. And the list of medical marvels goes on and on.

You may have a chronic illness, and even though the newest experimental medicines can't completely cure it, they may go a long way to making it manageable.

It's wise to see a doctor when you are sick, and the Bible doesn't indicate that believers are to seek only miraculous healing. But there is still much that even the best doctors don't know. So while consulting them, you must also look to the Lord. He is the ultimate healer.

King Asa looked for help only from physicians and failed to seek God—even when his disease became severe. As a result, he died. This is not to "dis" modern medicine, however, but simply to remind you to look to God.

Lord, I am grateful for trained physicians. Guide their hands and
give them wisdom for treating patients like me. However, I know that
ultimately, healing rests in Your hands, so I look to You for my healing
whether it is by a miracle or through modern medicine. Amen.

Death of a Child

Mourning a Child

"While the child was alive, I fasted and wept. . . . But now he is dead."
2 SAMUEL 12:22–23 NKJV

David had a child by Bathsheba, but he had committed adultery with her and had her husband murdered, so God told him that the child would die. When the infant became sick, David fasted and wept. But because God had made His will clear, David accepted the fact when the baby passed away.

Usually, however, the reasons for a child's death aren't clear, and you are left in grief, wondering why God took him or her. Losing a child is a very painful experience. It's almost never a consequence of your sin, but you may feel that God has acted cruelly or without reason.

It's often easier to accept the death of a parent who has lived a full life than it is to see a child die before having an opportunity to experience what life on earth has to offer. One question burns in your mind: *Why?* And there usually doesn't seem to be an acceptable answer.

God understands your grief, but He also knows that you will have great joy when you are reunited with your child in heaven.

Father, You know what it is like to lose a child to death.
I don't understand why this has happened to my child.
I need Your mercy and compassion, but most of all I need
Your presence as I struggle in my pain and grief. Amen.

When Your Child Dies

Some time later the woman's son became sick.
He grew worse and worse, and finally he died.

1 KINGS 17:17 NLT

Many a parent has passed sleepless nights watching over a child with a terminal illness. You endure agony as you watch them pass "through the valley of the shadow of death" (Psalm 23:4 KJV). And the pain is overwhelming when he or she finally leaves this life.

It's very difficult to say goodbye. And the days that follow have even more pain. You sit silently in his room, trying to grasp that he is truly gone. You arrange her toy animals on her bed, as if that might somehow make some sense of all the pain.

But try as you might, it makes no sense. What could be the purpose in taking such a beautiful child? But just as with Enoch, God has His reasons. "Enoch lived in close fellowship with God. . . . Then one day. . .God took him" (Genesis 5:22, 24 NLT).

Only time will heal your heartache—that and the knowledge that your child is now running through bright fields of splendor above, totally, unreservedly happy.

God, in my mind I know my child is healthy and happy in heaven with You, but my heart only feels the grief of separation. I need Your loving arms around me as I walk through this valley of loss. Amen.

Jairus' Daughter

We all eventually die, and when someone's time has come to leave this life, we do well to accept it. But that isn't easy when the person whose time has come is very young and hasn't yet experienced all that life has to offer.

The New Testament records Jesus raising the dead on three occasions: He revived a young man, He brought a twelve-year-old girl back to life, and He raised His friend Lazarus (Luke 7:14–15; 8:51–55; John 11:38–44, respectively). Raising the dead was an exception, even for Jesus. Many hundreds of people died in Israel during the time of Jesus' ministry, and they didn't return.

But when someone dies with faith in Jesus, they live forever in His heavenly kingdom. This life is not the end, and the Bible refers to their temporary absence as "sleeping" (1 Corinthians 15:51; 1 Thessalonians 4:14). One day God will wake them, and their physical bodies will be resurrected in eternal life.

In that day, you and your departed child shall live together once again in rapturous joy.

Lord, even though it is hard to see it right now, I am grateful that death is not the end. Thank You for an eternity in heaven with You and those I love. In the meantime, I need You to be my comfort. Amen.

With You a Short Time

"Never again will there be in it an infant who lives but a few days."
ISAIAH 65:20 NIV

Jesus once described a woman suffering the pains of labor: "When her child is born, her anguish gives way to joy because she has brought a new baby into the world" (John 16:21 NLT). After nine months of pregnancy, parents are delighted to welcome a new life.

But sometimes that joy is short-lived. Even though the infant mortality rate is very low in the West, children still die in their first months. This raises painful questions: Why was this new life given, only to be snatched away? And the inevitable question: *What did I do wrong?*

It's usually not that you did anything wrong. God isn't judging you for some sin. It's just that life is often hard. People in developing nations face this grim reality on a much more frequent basis. But one day such sorrow will be no more in all the earth.

During the coming reign of Christ on earth, "the child shall die one hundred years old" (Isaiah 65:20 NKJV) after living a full, happy life.

Father, I know that death is a reality in this world, but I still struggle with the loss and why this has happened. I don't know why my baby had such a short life, but I need Your comfort. Help me to find peace even when I don't understand. Amen.

Death of a Parent
The Passing of a Parent

I bowed down heavily, as one who mourns for his mother.
PSALM 35:14 NKJV

No matter how many signs you have of a parent's approaching death, even if he or she has been in failing health for years, the time of death can still come as a shock. It's the finality of it—knowing that you will never hear your father tell another corny joke or your mother express joy over another simple gift.

The grandfather clock still ticks away, but your parent's chair is now empty. Everywhere you look you find memories—from the photo albums, to the pictures on the walls, to the unfinished woodworking projects in his garage or the half-knitted sweater in her sitting room.

Your mind is numb, and it takes the actual funeral for the reality to sink in that your parent is gone. Your days are filled with kind faces and gentle voices speaking condolences, but with every night come the emptiness and the tears.

You know your parent is with God now, and you know that must be incredibly beautiful, but you still need time to deal with your grief.

Lord, I know my parent is with You in heaven, but I am struggling with their absence. Be with me and comfort me when grief suddenly overtakes me at odd moments. Help me to walk this path of loss. Amen.

On to a Heavenly Reward

Then he breathed his last and died at a ripe
old age, joining his ancestors in death.
GENESIS 35:29 NLT

Isaac lived to a great age, and when he passed away, his sons, Esau and Jacob, came to bury him. All his household mourned him. But Isaac had died "at a ripe old age," having lived a long, eventful life for God. The passing of this great man was as much an occasion to celebrate his legacy as it was to mourn his death.

Isaac had been fading for years—likely for decades—so his death came as no surprise. The passing away of your parents may be similar. They may even have had "a desire to depart and be with Christ" (Philippians 1:23 NKJV).

In fact, since Jesus opened the way to heaven, the demise of any born-again senior saint is cause for celebration. Although you will certainly miss your loved ones, it is comforting to know that if they loved the Lord they have gone on to a well-deserved reward. It's wonderful to realize that they are finally home, thronged by a company of great saints of ages past who have gone there before them.

Father, I am mourning the loss of my parent's presence,
but I know that they are in heaven with You and I will
join them one day. In the meantime, I need Your strength
and comfort each day as I await that day. Amen.

Grieving a Mother

He married Rebekah and. . .he loved her. So Isaac
found comfort after his mother's death.
GENESIS 24:67 MSG

When Sarah died, Abraham mourned and wept bitter tears. But Abraham wasn't the only one in mourning. His son Isaac also grieved. He was the only son of his mother, and they'd had a special bond. So for months after her death, he found no comfort.

Abraham took another wife named Keturah, and he wisely realized that it was time that his son got married. So he sent a servant to Haran, and soon Rebekah came riding back in the camel caravan. After he was married, Isaac found solace, sweet companionship, and a sympathetic ear in Rebekah.

When your mother dies, you will probably feel emptiness within—even if you weren't as close to her as Isaac was to his mother. And though life must go on, there may be a mantle of grief draped over your days for some time.

Be sure to reach out to others who understand your sorrow and can sympathize and weep with you (Romans 12:15). It's important to process your grief, not bottle it all up inside.

Father, only You truly know my sorrow and grief,
but there are others whom You have put in my path
who have experienced similar loss. Help me to share my
feelings and accept their help in processing my grief. Amen.

A Ripe Sheaf of Grain

"You shall come to the grave at a full age,
as a sheaf of grain ripens in its season."
JOB 5:26 NKJV

A long life lived for God is a beautiful thing. The departure to heaven of an aged saint is a joyful event. For when they finally arrive in their eternal home, they will hear, "Well done, good and faithful servant" (Matthew 25:21 NKJV).

The Bible describes the death of a senior saint in delightful terms: if they die at a "full age," crowned with a head of white hair, scripture says they are like a sheaf of grain that has ripened at the end of the long summer season. Then the long-awaited harvest comes and they are taken home. Of course, their passing is bittersweet for those left behind, but death for a Christian is not the end.

It's right and proper to mourn the passing of an elderly believer, but it is also appropriate to celebrate a life well lived and to focus on the legacy the person leaves. This is true even if the person didn't accomplish "great" things but was simply a faithful husband or wife and a loving grandparent.

Lord, I am grateful that I know You have welcomed my loved
one home to heaven and that they are celebrating in Your
presence. Though I miss them, I know I will see them again
one day, but be my comfort in the meantime. Amen.

Death of a Spouse

Loss of a Forever Love

Then Elimelech died, and Naomi was left with her two sons.
RUTH 1:3 NLT

Once when there was a long famine in Israel, Naomi and her husband left Bethlehem for Moab, where they found some relief for a few years. There Naomi's husband died. Naomi was grief-stricken, and none of her relatives and former neighbors were present to comfort her.

To make matters worse, her two sons died also. This left her financially destitute. A devastated widow, she decided to return to Israel. As she went, she lamented, "The LORD's hand has turned against me!" (Ruth 1:13 NIV).

Many people down through the centuries have identified with Naomi's feelings of despair. It is very difficult to lose a life partner, and it is worse when you have to take over your deceased spouse's duties and handle the finances.

But we know the end of Naomi's story: God showed her tender compassion. Her daughter-in-law Ruth had returned with her to Judah, married a wealthy landowner, and cared for her. Naomi had thought that God had abandoned her. . .but He hadn't. He hasn't abandoned you either.

Father, I feel lost and alone. It feels like You have abandoned me, but I know You said You would never leave me nor forsake me, so I will trust You. Let me feel Your comforting arms around me. Amen.

Mourning a Life Companion

Sarah died. . .and Abraham came to mourn for Sarah, and to weep for her.
GENESIS 23:2 KJV

Sarah lived for 127 years, so she and Abraham had been married for about 110 years. Sarah was very beautiful and maintained her lovely features into her senior years. We know this because the king of Gerar desired to marry her when she was ninety (Genesis 17:17; 20:1–2).

When Sarah died, Abraham wept openly. She had been his closest companion for more than a century. Then, cloaked in his grief, he took care of funeral arrangements. It was at this time that he bought the cave of Machpelah for a family tomb.

When your life's companion dies, it seems that part of you dies as well. You had "become one" in marriage, and your physical beings, emotions, and habits had become almost inextricably intertwined, so much so that you can be at a loss as to how you will cope. This is different from the loss of a friend or even another family member.

At such times, the knowledge that you will see your loved one again in heaven gives steady light for your path.

God, I know I will see my love again one day, but in the meantime, I am struggling. I need Your comfort and guidance as I try to find a new normal one day at a time. Help me to find my way forward. Amen.

The Desire of Your Eyes

*"Behold, I take away from you the
desire of your eyes with one stroke."*
EZEKIEL 24:16 NKJV

Ezekiel was a young priest, and like many other Jewish captives, he was living in exile in Babylon. But he had one consolation: he was very happily married and his wife was "the desire of [his] eyes." Then one morning God warned Ezekiel that He was about to take her.

The Bible doesn't indicate whether Ezekiel's wife was already sick from a lingering disease—and whether she took a turn for the worse, prompting this revelation—or whether she suffered from a sudden, unexpected stroke. But that same evening she died.

God gave Ezekiel a very unusual command, instructing him not to mourn outwardly, but to "sigh in silence" (24:17 NKJV). And Ezekiel obeyed. If his wife had been sick for many months, this would have given him time to prepare for her eventual demise, but still, Ezekiel would have been very heavyhearted.

It is especially difficult when your spouse dies young, in the prime of life. God understands your sorrow and expects you to grieve. His command to Ezekiel was a rare exception.

---

*Father, I know life isn't always fair and everyone dies,
but I am struggling to understand why. Help me. My
heart is broken and only You can heal it. Teach me to
trust You even when I don't understand. Amen.*

Depression

Refusing to Despair

*We are pressed on every side by troubles, but we are not
crushed. We are perplexed, but not driven to despair.*

2 Corinthians 4:8 nlt

The apostle Paul endured unbelievable hardships yet kept a positive
outlook. In Philippi, he and Silas were cruelly beaten and thrown
into prison. Instead of complaining, they sang praise to God (Acts
16:22–25). Paul refused to give in to despair and later advised the
persecuted Philippian believers, "Rejoice in the Lord always. Again
I will say, rejoice!" (Philippians 4:4 nkjv).

Many modern Christians, however, suffer from depression, and
though they battle it and seek to stay positive, they are not always
successful. Instead of berating them for being too weak to maintain
a victorious attitude, we should commend them for their efforts and
encourage them to continue trusting God.

If you suffer from clinical depression, you may sometimes feel
helpless to rise above dark waves of depression. Don't feel condemned if you need to seek therapy and/or take medication to adjust
a chemical imbalance in your brain.

At the same time, aggressively strive to be positive—soaking
your thoughts in God's Word, listening to praise and worship music,
and constantly quoting faith-building promises from scripture.

---

*Lord, when I am in a dark moment, bring to my
mind Your Word as I battle through, and help me to find
the best way to handle these thoughts and feelings that
overwhelm me. Show me how to gain the victory. Amen.*

Reason to Live

"What strength do I have, that I should hope?
And what is my end, that I should prolong my life?"
JOB 6:11 NKJV

Depression can have many causes, but when it comes, it can sap your will to live. You don't feel like doing anything. Everything seems hopeless. And sometimes there may not be much you can do—particularly if you have a physical disability that leaves you with little strength or bedridden.

You may wonder why you should continue to hope. What strength do you have to act even if an opportunity were to open? What is God's plan, what end does He have in mind, that you should continue hoping? What could He possibly still have for you to accomplish, given the state you are in?

If you feel there is no reason to live, you may desire to depart for heaven before God is done with you on earth. But God doesn't see the way people see. What to you may seem like large, meaningful accomplishments—causes well worth living for—may have little significance to God. But small, everyday acts that seem almost insignificant to you may be vitally important to Him.

Lord, help me to see the value of even seemingly little victories,
like getting out of bed and taking a shower. I know You have
good plans for me even though I can't see them right now.
Give me strength to keep moving forward until I can. Amen.

A Crushed Spirit

My heart is smitten, and withered like grass;
so that I forget to eat my bread.
PSALM 102:4 KJV

You can bear up under great adversity as long as you have hope. You can suffer setbacks and sicknesses or endure rejection as long as you keep your spirits up. But once you lose hope, you succumb to depression. "The human spirit can endure in sickness, but a crushed spirit who can bear?" (Proverbs 18:14 NIV).

The Bible tells us that "a broken spirit dries the bones" (Proverbs 17:22 NKJV). Sometimes you feel hopeless and dispirited, with no will to continue. You are unable to go on.

If you are suffering from depression, the source of your pain may be a broken spirit. Life has battered you badly, shaking your trust in God, and drained your will to continue. And if you had a preexisting disposition to depression, it has hit you all the harder.

Rest in the Lord and let Him renew you. Meditate on His Word and draw strength from His promises. Allow His gentle hands to mend your wounds and restore your confidence.

Father, restore my spirit. Bring Your Word to my mind
so that I might remember Your goodness and power.
You alone are my hope. Help me to rest in Your love
as You give me wings like the eagle. Amen.

A Broken Spirit

Faith in God will keep you going even when you are sick. But if you lose all hope, if your spirit is weak and broken, nothing remains to sustain you. Then you are left with depression.

Many Christians mistakenly think that God wants them to be desperate, broken, and weeping, for they wrongly translate David's words, "The LORD is close to the brokenhearted and saves those who are crushed in spirit" (Psalm 34:18 NIV). However, He draws near you to heal your broken spirit and comfort you—not to make you broken.

Throughout the scriptures, being broken means being shattered (Jeremiah 19:1–2, 10–11) and crushed and weak (Proverbs 15:13; 17:22). Breaking is what happens to dry, brittle, hardened vessels that can no longer be changed, for which there is no more hope.

But if you are a moist, soft clay vessel, still trusting God, still on the potter's wheel, He allows pressure to mold and shape you. This pressure may be painful at times, but it leads to godly change, not hopelessness and depression.

Lord, You said You are near to the brokenhearted and
will comfort them. I come to You brokenhearted. I need
Your comfort and healing. Draw me near to You so that
I can feel Your loving arms around me. Amen.

A Comforting Friend

*It was a beautiful thing that you
came alongside me in my troubles.*
PHILIPPIANS 4:14 MSG

Many people don't have an actual case of clinical depression; nevertheless, they feel down and depressed. Perhaps life has dealt them a series of hard blows that have dampened their spirits and weighed them down. Or perhaps there is a cloud over their days because of worries about their health, their finances, or their families.

Taking the time to speak encouraging words to them can be a huge help. Solomon said, "Anxiety in the heart of man causes depression, but a good word makes it glad" (Proverbs 12:25 NKJV).

You may hesitate to try to encourage someone. You may think that you won't know what to say, that you will come off sounding awkward, or that your words won't have any effect. Go ahead and do it anyway. Your friend will probably appreciate that you cared enough to try.

Sometimes just coming alongside someone helps, even if you don't have great words of wisdom to impart. They will be glad to know that you are thinking about them and praying for them.

---

*Holy Spirit, help me to know when to be silent and just
sit with my friend and when to spur them forward. Give me
the courage to speak the words You would have me say.
Guide me because only You know what they need. Amen.*

Disabilities

When Children Have Disabilities

His nurse picked him up and fled, but as she
hurried to leave, he fell and became disabled.

2 SAMUEL 4:4 NIV

It's difficult to understand why babies are born with disabilities. It's just as difficult to understand why God allows young children to suffer disease or accidents that leave them disabled for life. This causes parents to ask, "Why *her*, God? What did this innocent child ever do to deserve this?"

The answer is that the child didn't "deserve" it, but diseases and accidents are no respecters of persons, and even children aren't spared. So they are born blind, deaf, and disabled, and while this causes the parents grief and soul-searching at first, they eventually accept their children's limitations and learn to encourage them to reach their full potential just the same.

But don't forget: God will one day utterly change them. Their present bodies may be weak or disabled, but when His kingdom comes, their bodies will be transformed and made powerful and eternal. "Our bodies are buried in brokenness, but they will be raised in glory. They are buried in weakness, but they will be raised in strength" (1 Corinthians 15:43 NLT).

Father, I don't understand why this has happened to an innocent child,
but understanding won't change the circumstances. Instead, help me
to make the most of my time by loving and encouraging my child until
the day we all stand in Your presence whole and healed. Amen.

Caring for Those with Disabilities

"When you give a banquet, invite the poor, the crippled, the lame, the blind, and you will be blessed."
LUKE 14:13–14 NIV

You may observe people gently caring for those with physical or mental disabilities and think, *So much love! I could never do that.* You may admire their dedication but not be able to imagine rolling up your sleeves and caring for those with disabilities yourself.

But caring for the poor, the disabled, the lame, the blind, and the mentally challenged can often be part of living the gospel. Jesus cares for them, and He tells you who follow Him to help the disadvantaged: "Whenever you did one of these things to someone overlooked or ignored, that was me—you did it to me" (Matthew 25:40 MSG).

Such loving actions begin at home—caring for a family member with disabilities, feeding an elderly parent, or spending time talking with a shut-in relative who tells you the same stories every time you visit.

If you yourself are disabled, you know how much such care and acts of kindness mean. So go the extra mile and show the same love to those less fortunate than you.

God, open my eyes to those around me that I may see them as You see them, love them as You love them, and serve them in Your name. May I do for others as I would have done for me. Amen.

Levites with Disabilities

"No man who has any defect may come near:
no man who is blind or lame, disfigured or deformed."
LEVITICUS 21:18 NIV

The law of Moses stated that no Levite who was "blind or lame, disfigured or deformed" could offer food to God on His altar. Some readers therefore conclude that God thinks less of those with disabilities, and they wonder why a God of love would reject human beings with disabilities—whom He Himself formed.

But God's love and care extend to those with disabilities, for in the same passage, the Lord said, "He may eat the most holy food of his God, as well as the holy food; yet because of his defect, he must not. . .approach the altar" (Leviticus 21:22–23 NIV).

Levites with disabilities could eat the food dedicated to God Almighty, including "the most holy food"—which was off limits to the vast majority of Israelites. God did not care less for them just because they weren't permitted to do everything able-bodied Levites did.

And now that Christ has opened the way to the Father, this restriction is past, and God's disabled children freely approach His throne of grace.

Jesus, because of Your sacrifice, everyone can come freely to
Your throne of grace. We are all broken and in need of Your
grace, mercy, and love, which are available to whosoever
will come, and You will hear their requests. Amen.

Healing and Helping

He looked up and said, "I see men like trees, walking."
MARK 8:24 NKJV

When Jesus came to Bethsaida, people brought a blind man to Him. Instead of immediately healing him, Jesus led him away from the crowds. Then He spit on his eyes, placed His hands on him, and asked him if he saw anything.

The man replied, "I see men like trees, walking." So Jesus placed His hands on the man's eyes again and made him look up. This time he saw everyone clearly. These days if someone saw men that blurry, most Christians would refer him to the optometrist.

In fact, medical missionaries, lacking the ability to miraculously heal the visually impaired, equip them with glasses or perform eye operations to correct their vision. And instead of healing paraplegics, practical Christians motivated by love provide wheelchairs to give them mobility.

It's great if you have the faith to heal the blind, the paralyzed, and the disabled, but few Christians actually have faith like that. But we should all have the love of Christ. And remember, it is even more even important to have love than the faith to work miracles (1 Corinthians 13:2, 13).

God, You do miracles every day. Sometimes it is through a miraculous healing, and sometimes it is through the work of trained medical personnel. Use me to be a conduit of Your love to others and serve their needs in Your name. Amen.

God's Children with Disabilities

*"Who makes the mute, the deaf, the seeing,
or the blind? Have not I, the LORD?"*

EXODUS 4:11 NKJV

You may have proclaimed this verse when a baby was born: "I praise you because I am fearfully and wonderfully made; your works are wonderful" (Psalm 139:14 NIV). But are God's works still wonderful when a child is born blind or with another imperfection? Yes, they are.

You may wonder what purpose the Lord has in creating the mute, the deaf, and the blind. But you do well to remember that all human beings are imperfect in one way or another—often in many ways. What is God's purpose in creating us?

Well, our lives owe much of their significance to how we affect others. People with disabilities have a powerful effect on people. They present countless opportunities to others to show compassion. When you love and help others, you fulfill Christ's law. "Carry each other's burdens, and in this way you will fulfill the law of Christ" (Galatians 6:2 NIV).

When we get to heaven, we will see how backward we had so many of our priorities, for "the last shall be first" (Matthew 19:30 KJV).

Father, we are all fearfully and wonderfully made in Your image. None of us are perfect, but we all have a role to play in serving You. Help me to do whatever You ask for even the least of these, for they are great in Your eyes. Amen.

75

Disappointment

Unrelenting Disappointment

Unrelenting disappointment leaves you heartsick,
but a sudden good break can turn life around.

God knows that relentless disappointment leaves you mentally exhausted. After a while, you begin to get the feeling that nothing good will ever come your way again. You are overcome with futility.

You may feel like Job, whose friends tried to encourage him that if he would hang in there, just persevere, God would eventually bless him again (Job 4:3–7; 8:6, 21). God would "restore to you the years that the. . .locust has eaten" (Joel 2:25 NKJV).

But like Job, you may have nearly given up hope that this will ever happen. When the locusts have devoured so many years of your life and you are persuaded that God Himself is intent on causing you grief, it is difficult to think that it will ever seem like a good idea to Him to bless you again.

But this time of testing and disappointment won't last forever. It too will pass. God loves you and is determined to do good in your life. Like the sun bursting through the clouds, He will completely change your situation and give you hope again.

Lord, Your Word says that weeping will endure for a
night but joy comes in the morning. Help me to endure the
struggle until morning comes and restores my joy once again.
My hope for a better tomorrow is in You alone. Amen.

Dealing with Disappointment

*"The brook vanishes in the heat. The caravans turn
aside to be refreshed, but there is nothing to drink."*

JOB 6:17–18 NLT

In Bible lands, intermittent brooks—called *wadis*—run with water
only after the spring rains. Then, as the long, hot summer months
stretch on, the streambeds dry up. Soon water is to be found only in
a few small pools. Many a caravan has stopped at a wadi, desperate
for water, to find nothing at all.

Perhaps you have experienced similar disappointment: You were
depending on a job to come through. You had exhausted all your
other resources and had no backup plan. You needed this to happen.
Yet it fell through, and you were bitterly disheartened.

What can you do? The Bible describes the arid valley of Baca.
Baca means "weeping" and symbolizes times of great disappointment. Yet God's people "passing through the valley of Baca make
it a well" (Psalm 84:6 KJV). When you desperately need water but
there is none in sight, that is when you must dig a well.

God will never fail you, but sometimes you need to dig deep in
a place of disappointment to find hope.

---

*God, when I look around, my life seems dry like a desert,
but You said You can make streams even in the wasteland.
Help me to dig deep in faith, knowing that You
are able to do what You said. Amen.*

When Hopes Are Dashed

They count on it but are disappointed.
When they arrive, their hopes are dashed.
JOB 6:20 NLT

When you are counting on someone to help you, but the time comes and your would-be helper bails out, your hopes are dashed. Maybe he promised to lend you money to meet an unexpected shortfall, or she said she would drive you to an appointment, but then the person doesn't come through.

God knows what it is like to be disappointed. He compared His care for Israel to a farmer painstakingly preparing the ground, removing stones, and planting a vineyard. Yet the vine produced bitter grapes. God asked, "What more could have been done to My vineyard that I have not done in it? Why then, when I expected it to bring forth good grapes, did it bring forth wild grapes?" (Isaiah 5:4 NKJV).

People continue to disappoint God today, yet He patiently, lovingly continues to work in their lives. "For He knows our frame; He remembers that we are dust" (Psalm 103:14 NKJV).

When your hopes fall through, look to God to comfort you and meet your needs. He will come through for you when people fail.

Father, my expectation comes from You and You alone.
When others fail me, I can count on You. Help me to give
grace and forgiveness to those who disappoint me, and help
me to trust wholly in You to provide for my needs. Amen.

Hope That Never Disappoints

This hope will not lead to disappointment.
For we know how dearly God loves us.

ROMANS 5:5 NLT

We all have had high hopes at times and have had our hearts set on something, only to be disappointed. People forget their promises or thoughtlessly fail to keep their word, and even "sure deals" fall through. Problems and trials seem to be woven right into the fabric of life and are constantly upsetting our carefully made plans.

But Paul said that it is not only possible to endure when you run into problems, but to rejoice, because trials develop godly character (Romans 5:3–4). This development process strengthens your confident hope of salvation, and such hope will never lead to disappointment.

Sometimes it is helpful to take a deep breath, pause for a moment, and see disappointments in perspective. This life is full of frustrations and failures, but through them all, God works everything for good and will more than make up for your losses in heaven.

You can be certain of this, knowing how much God loves you. This love is what moves Him to have so many wonderful things planned and waiting for you. And God never disappoints.

God, even when my plans fail and people disappoint me,
I know that Your plans will always come to pass. You will
never disappoint me. Help me to keep my focus on You and
to have patience to wait on Your plan for my life. Amen.

Disappointing Returns

"You looked for much, but indeed it came to little."
HAGGAI 1:9 NKJV

How many times have you launched out on a new venture with high hopes, only to have your hopes dashed? Many times, if you are an entrepreneur. This can be very upsetting after putting your all into something.

You realize that in the past you have gone off half-cocked, so this time you do lots of research, come up with a truly winning idea, and carefully plan all the details—only to fail again.

As the prophet Haggai explained, this often happens if you don't put God and His purposes first. As a result, He isn't with you to bless you. But it can also happen for inscrutable marketing reasons, and often there is no way to accurately predict what will succeed. The Bible says, "For you do not know which will prosper, either this or that" (Ecclesiastes 11:6 NKJV).

As Solomon noted, "The race is not to the swift. . .nor riches to men of understanding, nor favor to men of skill; but time and chance happen to them all" (Ecclesiastes 9:11 NKJV). Often that is just the way things are.

---

*Father, when things don't work out the way I want them to,
I know You are still at work because You can even use failures
to strengthen my character and prepare me for future work in
Your kingdom. Help me to use failure as a time of growth. Amen.*

Dishonesty

Live Honestly

*"Live in the fear of GOD—be most careful,
for GOD hates dishonesty, partiality, and bribery."*

2 CHRONICLES 19:7 MSG

Human nature is predictable: it always seeks comfort, pleasure, and plenty and avoids difficulty, pain, and loss. That is why people are so often tempted to cut corners at work or to fudge numbers when charging customers or paying taxes. Sometimes it seems that dishonesty is the default setting of mankind.

Partiality is another way of bending the rules. While you may be convinced that you treat everyone the same, do you show favorites by allowing certain people privileges, access, and leniency that you don't offer to others?

And while you might be dismayed at the blatant bribery in third-world countries, it is nevertheless alive (in its more polite forms) in our own country. For example, are you more inclined to do things promptly and well for people who have shown favors to you or scratched your back in some way?

The best way to avoid dishonesty and partiality is to revere God and seek to please Him. Then He will help you to be honest in all your dealings with others.

---

*Holy Spirit, search me and try me. Show me where I fail
to be impartial or honest. May I keep Jesus as my goal
for how to live my life and not compare myself to other
people. I want to please You and not men. Amen.*

Honesty and Dishonesty

Honesty guides good people;
dishonesty destroys treacherous people.
PROVERBS 11:3 NLT

Picture yourself traveling through unfamiliar territory in the dark. The path has many forks, and you have no idea which way to choose. Would you be happy if someone who knows that region like the back of his hand offered to guide you to your destination? Of course!

Life itself is often dark, unfamiliar territory. But you can know that you are walking on the right path if you have honesty guiding your steps.

Many times, if you choose what is honest, you seem to be losing out—while unscrupulous, crooked people who take devious shortcuts get ahead in life. But you avoid many pitfalls by having integrity. For one thing, if you both get audited, he is the one who suffers.

And if you consistently own up to your mistakes instead of trying to wiggle out of any responsibility, you will gain a reputation for honesty. This will serve you well.

It may take a while, sometimes years, but dishonesty eventually destroys those foolish enough to indulge in it. "Better to be poor and honest than to be dishonest and a fool" (Proverbs 19:1 NLT).

Lord, grant me the strength to follow the right path
and to live honestly in dealing with myself and others.
The path may seem hard at times, but it is easier because
You walk beside me. I trust the outcome to You. Amen.

Principles of Honesty

How you handle dimes and dollars is a very good indicator of how you will handle a much larger amount. You might think that small sums of money aren't significant—it is all slush fund until it reaches a certain threshold. But God watches how honest you are with pocket change before He trusts you with more.

The aggregate effect of small, corrupt money habits carries a huge price tag. Even a small hole will eventually sink a large ship. The continual dripping of a leaky faucet will, over time, drain your tank dry. And as Solomon put it, "the little foxes. . .ruin the vineyards" (Song of Songs 2:15 NIV).

Besides, if you are used to spending money recklessly and aren't on the level with small sums, your habits will continue unchanged if you come into a large amount of money. You will be even more likely to fudge on your tax forms with big sums of money.

Determine to be scrupulously honest. Doing so may require a constant focus for some time, but eventually you will form new habits.

---

*Father, help me to develop good habits, especially with
the small things in my life, because I know they add up
in the long run. I want to build a godly character that
will glorify You in my day-to-day walk. Amen.*

Entirely Honest

They must not. . .steal, but must show themselves
to be entirely trustworthy and good.
TITUS 2:9–10 NLT

Many people who wouldn't think of stealing even a piece of candy from a corner store feel no compunction against taking materials or supplies from their workplace. Or they make false statements on their tax forms to save hundreds of dollars.

This attitude seems to have particular appeal if life has dealt them some hard or unfair financial blows. They then reason that they are just "evening things up." Take this one step further and they refuse to speak up if a department store undercharges them $50 for an item. They reason that it is the store's job, not theirs, to catch such things. So much for being too honest to steal a piece of candy.

Often, however, people start off being dishonest with small amounts and progress to being dishonest with larger sums. This is why Christians are to be *"entirely* trustworthy and good" (emphasis added)—honest in that which is least and honest in that which is much.

Make up your mind before temptation strikes that you are going to be honest no matter what the temptation is.

Holy Spirit, show me when I am tempted to be dishonest
even in the smallest of matters because it can become a bad
habit that can lead to a road of destruction. Help me to
keep my spirit clean and my conscience clear. Amen.

Dishonest Gain

Dishonest money dwindles away, but whoever
gathers money little by little makes it grow.
PROVERBS 13:11 NIV

What do you do when crooked businesspeople prosper all around you and never seem to get caught? Meanwhile, you work hard and operate honestly, but struggle to stay afloat—let alone get ahead. You can barely sock away enough funds to pay your taxes, and you often dread Christmas because it is a yearly reminder of how financially tight you are.

Judgment may not come suddenly on the dishonest, but their money often slowly bleeds from their bank accounts and dwindles away. But if you faithfully set a little aside—even if it isn't much—over time it grows.

Remember, however that this is a financial *principle*—true in most situations over time but not an ironclad promise that invariably comes to pass.

This fact remains: "Better the little that the righteous have than the wealth of many wicked" (Psalm 37:16 NIV). This is why James says, "Believers who are poor have something to boast about, for God has honored them" (James 1:9 NLT).

Lord, help me to be faithful even with little and make the most
of what I have been given. I know You will honor and grow
a faithful spirit that is obedient to Your will, but better a little
with Your blessing than great wealth without it. Amen.

Divorce/Separation

Rejected and Distressed

"The LORD will call you back as if you were a wife deserted and distressed in spirit—a wife who married young, only to be rejected."
ISAIAH 54:6 NIV

Divorce causes deep pain. If your marriage has ended, you understand this only too well. The emotional pain of such an experience can be excruciating—particularly if you wanted your marriage to continue but your spouse insisted on a divorce. It only compounds the pain if he or she angrily blamed you for all the "irreconcilable differences."

On your wedding day, you promised to be true, and in return, your loved one promised eternal love and faithfulness to you, and only you. That sacred trust has been broken, and to be rejected afterward in anger and bitterness is devastating.

"The LORD God. . .hates divorce" (Malachi 2:16 NKJV), and He hates it for all the same reasons you do. God feels your pain, and it grieves His heart to see you go through such emotional anguish. Also, He knows that the breakup of a marriage has other far-reaching repercussions, particularly if children are involved.

Your husband may have rejected you, but God will *never* reject you.

Father, my heart is broken, and I feel rejected and abandoned, but I know that even if my husband leaves, You have not left me. I am not alone as long as I have You. Be my comfort and stay. Amen.

God Still Loves You

"The fact is, you have had five husbands,
and the man you now have is not your husband."
JOHN 4:18 NIV

Samaritans held to the law of Moses, and one Samaritan woman took advantage of the fact that divorce was permitted to divorce and remarry several times. She eventually ended up just living with a man, something the law didn't sanction.

Most people in her town shunned her, which is why she came to the well alone in the heat of the day. But Jesus, who spoke clearly against divorce, had compassion on her and had a profound spiritual conversation with her. She very likely decided to legally marry her partner after Jesus' visit, but the point is this: if you have been through a divorce and feel condemned, if you feel like an outcast and a failure, if you wonder if God forgives you, remember Jesus' love and beautiful conversation with the Samaritan woman.

He didn't condemn her. Instead, He led her gently to living water and even used her to bring His truth to her town. God still loves you and longs to speak to you as well.

Lord, I feel like a failure. Please forgive me and help me
to move forward in Your will. I want to live a life that will
honor You. Show me how to walk in Your way from this
day forward because I don't want to go back. Amen.

When Love Isn't There

Then she said to him, "How can you say,
'I love you,' when your heart is not with me?"
JUDGES 16:15 NKJV

Sometimes you simply don't feel "in love" anymore. There are things you can do to rejuvenate caring and intimacy, but when you have let things slide for a long time, it takes a complete change of mind and a strong commitment to restore romance. And you may not feel up to it right now.

A temporary separation may be helpful. Paul wrote, "A wife must not separate from her husband. But if she does, she must remain unmarried or else be reconciled to her husband" (1 Corinthians 7:10–11 NIV). At times couples simply need a breather, a little space to think things through.

Often even a separation is unnecessary. When your heart isn't with your spouse anymore, you can't fake the rosy flush of love, but you can show kindness, thoughtfulness, and do small loving acts. And if you are intent on saving your marriage, you will keep at it.

If the other person doesn't respond immediately, don't give up. It can take a while to rekindle emotions of love.

Father, I made a commitment when I got married to love until
death do us part. Rekindle the flame of love in my marriage
and help me to be patient with my husband. Help me to
choose love every day, even when I don't feel it. Amen.

Doubt

Breaking Free from Disbelief

"Why do doubts rise in your minds?"
LUKE 24:38 NIV

Some people seem prone to doubting, trapped in a disbelieving mind-set. Even Jesus' disciples were often this way. After His resurrection, "He rebuked their unbelief and hardness of heart, because they did not believe" (Mark 16:14 NKJV). Some people, like Thomas, seem especially inclined to being skeptical.

If you realize your faith isn't strong and you don't have confidence that God will answer your prayers, you can take steps to increase your faith. First, you must earnestly desire greater faith and, like the disciples, plead, "Increase our faith" (Luke 17:5 NKJV). God will certainly answer such sincere requests, though it may take a while.

When God begins to increase your faith and you see your prayers being answered, then do all you can to encourage it. Paul wrote to Timothy, "Fan into flame the gift of God, which is in you" (2 Timothy 1:6 NIV). God had given Timothy a spiritual gift, and now that this gift was in Timothy's possession, he needed to stir it up, to fan the burning ember into a fire.

God, I want to believe, but I struggle with doubts and disbelief.
Help me to see You at work all around me. Remind me
of answered prayers, bring to my mind scriptures to hold
on to, and fan into flame the gift of faith. Amen.

Willing Disbelief

But though he had done so many miracles
before them, yet they believed not on him.

JOHN 12:37 KJV

Jesus was often disappointed that His disciples lacked faith. When they feared during a storm, He asked, "Why are you so afraid? Do you still have no faith?" (Mark 4:40 NIV). He asked again, "Where is your faith?" (Luke 8:25 NIV). He expected them to have more faith.

One time Jesus visited His hometown of Nazareth. Mark 6:2 (NIV) says that the people of Nazareth were "amazed" that Jesus exhibited such miraculous powers. For His part, "He was amazed at their lack of faith" (v. 6 NIV). Their faith was so unreasonably, stubbornly small because they were refusing to believe.

But you can choose to have faith. And when you have difficulty believing, you can pray, "Lord, I believe; help my unbelief!" (Mark 9:24 NKJV). The fact is, you *need* faith if you are to truly trust God and survive the storms of life.

No, you can't work up faith by your own efforts, but having the desire to trust God is an excellent place to start. Cry out to God today to increase your faith.

Lord, I am asking You to increase my faith because I
cannot do it alone. Block the distractions of the world
and remind me of the ways You have worked in my life
in the past. I believe, but help my unbelief. Amen.

Pleasing or Displeasing God

It's impossible to please God apart from faith.
HEBREWS 11:6 MSG

God loves faith—that is, *real* faith, not constant proclamations of faith when you are actually uncertain. The Bible says that it is impossible to please God if you don't have faith, and to have faith, you must trust Him. To trust Him, you must first come to the realization that God can be trusted.

You may be of a rational mind-set. Believing things without evidence doesn't come easy for you. That's not a problem. God doesn't expect you to jettison your brain and leap naively into the dark. He is willing to prove that He can be trusted (John 2:23; 14:29).

The catch is, once He provides proof, He expects you to transfer your trust to Him. But many people are unwilling to do so. "Although He had done so many signs before them, they did not believe in Him" (John 12:37 NKJV).

Jesus was willing to provide compelling evidence to doubting Thomas (John 20:26–28). He will do the same for you if you sincerely seek and ask (Matthew 7:7–8), but you must seek the Lord wholeheartedly, sincerely wanting to know the truth.

Lord, I am seeking You with my whole heart. I want a faith that is pleasing to You. Show me who You are and help me to trust that You will do what You say You will do by helping me see the evidence in my daily life. Amen.

Doubts Create Instability

If ye will not believe, surely ye shall not be established.
ISAIAH 7:9 KJV

God has made many clear promises in the Bible. He has promised that if you love and obey Him, He will protect you, He will provide all your needs, and He will be with you during times of trouble.

You need to do your part, to be sure. But if you do, you can then trust that God will keep His word and do His part. If, however, you feel that He is either unable or unwilling to do so, you have a breakdown in trust and communication. And as Isaiah said, "If ye will not believe, surely ye shall not be established."

You sometimes can't prevent being assailed by a barrage of doubts. Often the devil hurls "fiery darts" (Ephesians 6:16 NKJV) to try to shake you from your position and force you to retreat. At such times, you need to raise your shield of faith to deflect them.

Use the faith you do have "that you may be able to withstand in the evil day, and having done all, to stand" (Ephesians 6:13 NKJV). Do this and you will be established.

God, I want to be unshakeable in my belief. I lift up my shield of faith. Bring to my mind scripture from Your Word to help combat the fiery darts of doubt, and help me to stand firm against the assaults of the enemy. Amen.

Drug Abuse

Hallucinogenic Drugs

Reuben found some mandrakes in the field and
brought them home to his mother Leah.

GENESIS 30:14 MSG

One day Jacob's young son Reuben was wandering through the grain fields when he found some unusual plants: their roots appeared to be distorted human figures and had a pungent smell (Song of Solomon 7:13). Excited, he took them to his mother, who recognized them as mandrakes. According to local lore, it enhanced fertility.

Mandrakes also contain psychedelic properties and for millennia have been used in superstitious practices and pagan magic rituals. Just because the use of certain hallucinogenic plants is accepted, however, doesn't mean God's people should indulge in them.

Some people argue that God created plants such as mandrakes, marijuana, and psychedelic mushrooms then point out that the Bible says, "God saw everything that He had made, and indeed it was very good" (Genesis 1:31 NKJV). They then contend that God intended people to enjoy eating or smoking them.

But nature has clearly fallen and is now corrupt (Romans 8:21 NKJV). For example, mushrooms such as *Amanita phalloides* (death cap) are deadly poisonous. Clearly, God intends you to have the wisdom to avoid certain plants.

Holy Spirit, the world is full of temptations. Help me to be wise in what I allow into my body. Show me what is good and useful and what has negative consequences so that I can honor God with my body. Amen.

Defiling God's Temple

If anyone defiles the temple of God, God will destroy him.
For the temple of God is holy, which temple you are.
1 CORINTHIANS 3:17 NKJV

At first drugs are an exciting thrill. You never knew you could experience such things—the stresses and boredom of your daily life seem a million miles away. And the fact that they are illegal sometimes makes them seem even more desirable.

But drugs have a harsh long-term effect on your mind and body. The ecstasy you enjoy comes with an excessively high price tag. After a while, you need greater doses to achieve the same pleasurable feelings. Also, you can easily become addicted, with your body craving stimulation whenever you are not high.

If you are a Christian, the Spirit of God lives within you. Your body is His temple. If you willfully defile your body, God removes His protection from you and allows you to suffer the consequences of your actions. God destroys you by allowing you to destroy yourself. In addition, full recovery isn't guaranteed, even if you stop.

Your body is meant to be holy and dedicated to God, so don't vandalize it.

God, my body is Your temple where You abide. Help me
to avoid things that will hurt my body and cause You
grief. Give me wisdom so that I can keep the temple
clean and abide in peace with You. Amen.

Repenting of Drug Use

*They did not repent of their murders or their sorceries
or their sexual immorality or their thefts.*
REVELATION 9:21 NKJV

The word *sorceries* in the above passage comes from the Greek word *pharmakon*, which refers to drugs. (This is related to our modern word *pharmacy*, a drugstore.) So when the Bible says that people "did not repent of. . .their sorceries," it is saying that they refused to repent of their drug abuse.

When battling a drug addiction, people can't change themselves, but God does ask them to repent of it. Repenting is something they can do. They must be ashamed of and hate the sin; they must turn to God and plead for Him to change them and then cooperate with what He does in them.

When the transforming power of God's Spirit enters someone's life, He begins to make changes. If the person has truly turned to God, change will manifest. But she or he must abide in Christ to maintain this victory. "Prove by the way you live that you have repented of your sins and turned to God" (Matthew 3:8 NLT).

This doesn't necessarily mean that victory will come easily, but it will come.

---

*Holy Spirit, I don't want to be held in bondage to drugs
anymore. I ask You to come into my spirit and transform
me from the inside out no matter how long it takes.
Help me to endure until the victory is mine. Amen.*

Dysfunctional Relationships

Roots of Sibling Rivalry

When his brothers realized that their father loved him more than them, they grew to hate him—they wouldn't even speak to him.
GENESIS 37:4 MSG

Jacob loved Joseph more than his other sons because he was the son of Jacob's beloved wife Rachel. It's sometimes easy for modern parents as well to favor one child over another. You may do this without even realizing it. "But if you show favoritism, you sin" (James 2:9 NIV).

Showing favoritism engenders a sense of entitlement in the favored child and insecurity in the less favored child. . .thus setting the stage for sibling rivalry. Many adults trace the roots of dysfunctional family relationships back to childhood.

A parent's approval is vitally important to a child's emotional and spiritual well-being. It influences their understanding of God's love and acceptance, views that persist into adulthood. If you have unwittingly contributed to sibling rivalries, you can still make amends now by deliberately, consciously showing love and attention to all your children equally.

Father, help me to treat my children equally and begin to undo any damage my past behaviors may have caused so that peace can be restored to my family. Amen.

Responding to Bullying

*Peninnah would taunt Hannah and make fun
of her. . . . Year after year it was the same.*

1 SAMUEL 1:6–7 NLT

Long ago when customs were different, a man named Elkanah had two wives, Peninnah and Hannah. Peninnah had several sons, but Hannah was childless. That was hard enough, but to make matters worse, Peninnah continually taunted Hannah about it, making her life miserable. This situation went on for quite some time.

Some people aren't fully aware that their words are causing pain, but others know exactly what they are doing and derive pleasure from causing others anguish. They enjoy causing fear by veiled threats. Even if they call themselves believers, their actions are usually motivated by hatred, and they need to repent.

If you are a victim of constant taunting, talk to mature Christians about it. Often, shining light on a bully's behavior is enough to make him or her desist. Even though bullying is common, people are aware these days that harassment and uttering threats are illegal.

If reporting the situation doesn't fully resolve it, entrust your griefs to God. He is able to change things and to bring peace to you.

---

*Lord, You know my suffering, and You know I cannot handle
this alone. I ask for Your protection from bullying. Sustain
me and give me strength to endure until You intervene
on my behalf or send others to help me. Amen.*

Opposed by Family Members

"Those closest to you, your own brothers and cousins, are working against you."
JEREMIAH 12:6 MSG

The prophet Jeremiah had a tough time of it. He lamented, "Alas, my mother, that you gave me birth, a man with whom the whole land strives and contends! . . . Everyone curses me" (Jeremiah 15:10 NIV).

Jeremiah expected the nation to reject him, but he may have hoped that at least his family would be loyal to him. Nevertheless, even they turned against him. Jesus experienced the same thing. "Even His brothers did not believe in Him" (John 7:5 NKJV).

If you follow the Lord, you can expect opposition. Jesus warned, "A man's enemies will be the members of his own household" (Matthew 10:36 NIV). At the end of the day, this opposition can leave you very discouraged.

Some families are already very divided, even without faith in Jesus being factored in. Brothers and sisters are at each other's throats; people aren't talking to each other and backstab each other. God can change even dysfunctional families. But in the meantime, be aware that they oppose you, and don't leave yourself open to their attacks.

Father, I ask You to be at work in restoring my family. Give me wisdom and guide me in how to interact with them so that You will be glorified. Help me to be loving, but guard me against potential attacks. Amen.

Dysfunctional Families

Son dishonors father, daughter rises against her mother,
daughter-in-law against her mother-in-law.

MICAH 7:6 NKJV

The prophet Micah described a low point in Israel's history. It was a time of unprecedented greed and corruption, and the morals and the structure of society were collapsing. All the judges accepted bribes, and families and communities were breaking apart. Things had become so bad that Micah advised, "Do not trust in a friend" (7:5 NKJV), and said that "a man's enemies are the men of his own household" (7:6 NKJV).

There are many similarities to today, and for the same reasons: society is undergoing moral collapse. There is a widespread breakdown in families, not only with an unprecedented number of divorces, but also with divisions within families.

Some families have so much dysfunction and strife that the situation may seem to be hopeless. But in the midst of all this, God's solution remains the same: "Love your neighbor as yourself" (Matthew 22:39 NLT)—and this includes flesh-and-blood family members.

Some deep-rooted grievances and divisions may take time and effort before they disappear, but God's love and power are able to resolve even them.

God, there is conflict within my family. The enemy is trying
to break us apart, and only You can bring reconciliation.
Lead me in how to respond in love, but also give me
wisdom to avoid the traps of the enemy. Amen.

Ungovernable Children

*His father had never rebuked him by asking,
"Why do you behave as you do?"*

1 KINGS 1:6 NIV

David was Israel's greatest king, a man who loved God whole-heartedly, and God blessed and honored him mightily. "David. . .had not failed to keep any of the LORD's commands all the days of his life—except in the case of Uriah the Hittite" (1 Kings 15:5 NIV).

Some critics, however, insist that David was also a failure as a father since he never asked his son Adonijah, "Why do you behave as you do?" The behavior in question probably refers to Adonijah thinking that, as the oldest son, he should receive both the throne and Abishag (1 Kings 2:15–17 NIV). So he "put himself forward" (1 Kings 1:5 NIV).

Whether David failed or not, many parents do fail to discipline their children, leading them to become spoiled. This creates a dysfunctional relationship. Of course, some teens refuse to be rebuked. The Bible specifically addresses this, reminding children to obey their parents (Ephesians 6:1).

Parents are to discipline their children, but the Bible also points out that some children choose their own willful ways, despite correction (Deuteronomy 21:18–21).

Lord, help me to lead my children in Your ways and discipline them by Your Word. I will do my part, but I know that in the end I have to leave them in Your loving hands and trust You for the outcome. Amen.

Elderly Parents
Caring for Parents

*Their first responsibility is to show godliness at home
and repay their parents by taking care of them.*
1 TIMOTHY 5:4 NLT

For most of human history, people took it for granted that when their parents became elderly, they would take their parents into their homes and look after them. This understanding persists in many countries—and Paul says that such practical demonstrations of love should characterize Christians.

It's good that Christians give to missions or the poor, but "their *first* responsibility is to. . .their parents" (emphasis added). Remember Jesus' reproof to the Pharisees: "You say it is all right for people to say to their parents, 'Sorry, I can't help you. For I have vowed to give to God what I would have given to you.' In this way, you let them disregard their needy parents" (Mark 7:11–12 NLT).

This doesn't mean your parents have to live with you—although it may mean that. They could live in a seniors' home and be perfectly happy and content. But the point is, it is your responsibility to see to it that they *are* receiving adequate care and support. And you certainly should visit them regularly.

---

*God, I want to honor my parents. Show me how I can do a
better job of supporting them and making sure their needs
are met. Help me to love through both word and deed in
ways that will glorify You as well as honor them. Amen.*

A Crown of Glory

The silver-haired head is a crown of glory,
if it is found in the way of righteousness.
PROVERBS 16:31 NKJV

These days it is common for seniors to be great-grandparents and to live well into their eighties and nineties. In Bible times, people were told to respect the elderly. Moses, speaking for the Lord, commanded, "You shall rise before the gray headed and honor the presence of an old man" (Leviticus 19:32 NKJV).

When your parents grow old and their hair turns white or silver, they gain a distinguished look. And if they have faithfully served God, the Bible says their hair is "a crown of glory." It's as if they have become royalty. You should respect them even more.

However, as elderly parents' memory begins to fail and their advice comes from a past century, it is easy to ignore what they say. The Bible therefore commands people to show respect by performing such acts as rising to their feet when an elderly person enters a room.

You are to show respect to your parents even when you yourself are an adult.

Father, help me to be patient and loving to my parents as You have been patient and loving to me by giving me parents who led me in the way of righteousness, for which I will forever be grateful. Amen.

Respecting Elderly Parents

*Listen to your father, who gave you life, and do
not despise your mother when she is old.*
PROVERBS 23:22 NIV

Respecting your parents is easy when you are a child. They are the authority figures. But when you become a teen, you tend to rebel to establish your own identity. As a young adult, you reengage with them as equals but still respect them, usually because they are in the prime of life and continue to exhibit much wisdom.

But making the transition can be difficult when roles are reversed and your parents depend on you. When your parents are elderly, many of their decisions seem naive or stubborn, and you must patiently explain to them or override their decisions. Consequently, you may lose a measure of respect for their decision-making ability. This is inevitable, but don't get to the point that you despise them. Solomon wrote, "Listen to your father. . .and do not despise your mother."

Don't merely humor your parents. Truly respect them, even if you must now take the lead in decisions that affect them. Respecting them means honoring them and treating them with dignity.

---

*Lord, help me to find a balance between being a caregiver
to my parents as they age and showing respect and
love to them for all they have done for me. Help me
to honor them and glorify Your name. Amen.*

The Blessing of Old Age

"Men and women of ripe old age will sit in the streets of Jerusalem,
each of them with cane in hand because of their age."
ZECHARIAH 8:4 NIV

In ancient Israel, living a long life was considered a great blessing. However, today many seniors only count it a blessing if they also experience good health to enjoy their golden years. They look in dismay on becoming weak, being housebound, or even needing a cane or walker.

But these restrictions often come with the territory and are part of God's overall blessing of advanced age. Zechariah declares that a sign of God's blessing on Israel was if men and women of advanced age sat along the streets of Jerusalem, every one of them with a cane in hand.

Why were they sitting along the streets? Because they didn't have the energy to run around. So they sat and talked and minded their grandchildren (Zechariah 8:5). Why did all of them need canes? To help them walk. . .slowly.

Your aged parents' weakness need not detract from the blessing of God in their lives.

God, help me to remember that just because the elderly have
slowed their pace doesn't mean they don't have something
to offer. Help me to take the time to listen to their wisdom
and give them the honor they deserve. Amen.

Enemies

Beset by Enemies

Consider my enemies, for they are many;
and they hate me with cruel hatred.

PSALM 25:19 NKJV

Things are often difficult enough already, but sometimes people set themselves up as your enemies and go out of their way to make your life miserable. Paul warned that people would oppose you simply for being a Christian. "Everyone who wants to live a godly life in Christ Jesus will be persecuted" (2 Timothy 3:12 NIV).

Paul added, "Not that the troubles should come as any surprise to you. . . . It's part of our calling" (1 Thessalonians 3:3 MSG). But to expect troubles is one thing; to experience them on an unrelenting basis is quite another.

David prayed for God to consider his enemies because they were wearing him down, and there were many of them. He had practically wandered into a hornets' nest. It was enough to make him throw up his hands and quit.

David said elsewhere, "I had fainted, unless I had believed to see the goodness of the LORD" (Psalm 27:13 KJV). But he did believe that the Lord would be good to him. That is why he prayed for God's help.

Lord, it seems like the enemy surrounds me and there
is no escape, but I know You are always with me.
Protect me and fight for me, because I would faint if I
did not believe I would see Your goodness. Amen.

Attacks by Enemies

*My enemies would hound me all day, for there
are many who fight against me, O Most High.*

PSALM 56:2 NKJV

David wrote this complaint when he was fleeing from King Saul
and had been arrested by the Philistines. And after he escaped the
Philistines, he was back to staying ahead of Saul. David's own people,
the Israelites, were betraying him to Saul. He certainly had many
fighting against him.

David had done nothing wrong, yet he was on the run like a
fugitive. Do you ever feel that way? You try to do what's right but only
succeed in angering corrupt people. Instead of being commended
for the good you do, you create jealous enemies. Talk about being
misunderstood! Jesus also had many enemies, through no fault of
His own.

At times in your life you may face strong opposition. Like David,
your only hope of surviving will be to focus your thoughts steadfastly
on God and cry out to Him. Otherwise you will go under, because
nobody can take constant harassment and persecution.

Thank God for times of peace but be assured that He is also
with you during times of trouble.

---

*God, You said that when I chose to follow You that others
would despise me, but now I am surrounded. I need Your
intervention and Your presence now, or I will go under
from the pressure. You are my only hope. Amen.*

Whispering against You

All my enemies whisper together against me;
they imagine the worst for me.

PSALM 41:7 NIV

Often, your enemies aren't able to do anything to actually hurt you. But that won't stop them from gossiping about you and imagining the worst about you and for you.

When people have decided that you are a bad person, they think all your motives are bad. No matter what you do, they condemn you. You probably wish that such people would get on with their lives and quit trying to wreck yours. But you can't control their attitudes or behavior. You can only control your own.

Ask God to give you peace, and don't worry about them. Keep your heart free of hatred. Jesus said, "Love your enemies, bless them that curse you, do good to them that hate you, and pray for them which despitefully use you, and persecute you" (Matthew 5:44 KJV).

If you love your enemies and ignore the gossip that you hear them saying, "even if they accuse you of doing wrong, they will see your honorable behavior, and they will give honor to God" (1 Peter 2:12 NLT).

Father, people are lying and spreading false rumors about
me in order to ruin my reputation, but You know the truth.
You know my heart. Give me Your peace, and help me to love
and forgive them so that You may be glorified. Amen.

God Will Defend You

*"You must worship only the Lord your God. He is the
one who will rescue you from all your enemies."*
2 Kings 17:39 nlt

You must spend time in God's presence worshiping Him and acknowledging that He alone is God. It's not that He needs you to remind Him of this fact, however. He is already aware of it. He says, "I am the Lord, and there is none else, there is no God beside me" (Isaiah 45:5 kjv).

But it is important that you know that God is the only one true God as well. This is why God says, "Be still, and know that I am God" (Psalm 46:10 kjv). You need to truly know that He is the all-powerful God. When you know this, you have faith to ask Him to protect you.

If you have enemies who are committed to doing you harm, you need an even more powerful ally who is committed to guarding you from all your enemies. And you have such a friend. When your enemies attack, as they sometimes will, God will rise up to rescue you.

You worship God because He is worthy to be worshiped. . .but doing so also has powerful benefits.

---

*God, You are the one true God. When the enemy attacks,
help me to be still and remember that You are the only one
who can defend me and deliver me from harm. I know
You will rescue me. My hope is in You. Amen.*

God Rescues You

*"You won't be handed over to those men whom you have
good reason to fear. Yes, I'll most certainly save you."*
JEREMIAH 39:17 MSG

Baruch came from an influential family of scribes in Jerusalem, and
he served as a scribe for the prophet Jeremiah, writing down his
prophecies. But because he helped such an unpopular public figure,
he had many powerful enemies.

Baruch was aware that people wanted him dead. But God promised that no matter what political pressures were at work behind
the scenes, he wouldn't be handed over to them. God would most
certainly defend him.

God has made many, many promises in His Word to protect
His people. If He had said these things just once or twice, it might
be possible to misunderstand. But He has made it abundantly clear
that it is His will to protect you, and He repeatedly tells you not
to fear.

At one point, the Jews complained, "The LORD has forsaken me,
the Lord has forgotten me." But God replied, "Can a mother forget
the baby at her breast. . . ? Though she may forget, I will not forget
you!" (Isaiah 49:14–15 NIV).

---

*Lord, I know You have not forgotten me, and You have
promised to defend me against my enemies. Help me to
trust in You and fear not even when the circumstances seem
impossible, because with You all things are possible. Amen.*

Facing Death
The Land of No Return

*When a few years are come, then I shall
go the way whence I shall not return.*
JOB 16:22 KJV

When you were young, you probably felt you were nearly immortal. Death, when you even thought about it, was very far off. It was easy to joke about it. But as you get older, you take it more seriously. You finally realize that, yes, you will die one day and it will be final.

As a Christian, you know that you will go into the presence of the Lord, so death has lost much of its sting. But the best news is that when Jesus returns, your body will be resurrected in great glory and power. In that sense, you do return. But Job was right: you don't return in your weak mortal body once it dies.

You don't need to fear death. Still, dying is a serious matter, and it is understandable that you will feel sorrow at the thought of leaving loved ones and all that is familiar. And regarding your work, you may regret leaving certain tasks unfinished. So even the thought of going to heaven can be bittersweet.

---

*Father, I am Your child, so I don't have to fear death because it is
not the end. One day I will go to a land of no return where I will
have a glorified body and spend eternity in Your presence. Amen.*

What Awaits Beyond?

Then Abraham gave up the ghost, and died in a
good old age, an old man, and full of years.
GENESIS 25:8 KJV

In Abraham's day, people had little knowledge of what awaited after death. They envisioned a vague, shadowy realm called Sheol where ghosts lived in a dim twilight of existence—not really living at all. Was Abraham apprehensive about dying? He might have been.

Yet Abraham was so blessed that the millions of people who died after him were carried by angels into "Abraham's bosom" (Luke 16:22 KJV), a paradise full of light and comfort. Centuries later, Moses and Elijah came from this heavenly place and "appeared in glorious splendor" (Luke 9:30 NIV).

This was even before Jesus died on the cross and opened the way to the Father's throne in heaven. We who die now go directly into the presence of Christ. To be absent from the body is to be present with the Lord (2 Corinthians 5:8). For Christians, there is no uncertainty about what awaits after death.

Paul said, "I desire to depart and be with Christ, which is better by far" (Philippians 1:23 NIV).

Lord, when I leave this body, I will be present with Christ.
Nothing else will ever compare to this, so I will not fear
death because it means being at home in heaven
with You face-to-face for eternity. Amen.

Dying Grace

For this God is our God for ever and ever:
he will be our guide even unto death.

PSALM 48:14 KJV

The writer of Psalm 71 was growing older and becoming painfully aware of his frailty and mortality. He implored, "Do not cast me off in the time of old age. . . . When I am old and grayheaded, O God, do not forsake me" (Psalm 71:9, 18 NKJV).

God gives a beautiful response in Isaiah, saying, "Even to your old age and gray hairs I am he, I am he who will sustain you. I have made you and I will carry you" (Isaiah 46:4 NIV). Not only will God be with you when you grow old, but He will be with you right to your dying moment—and beyond! He will literally be your God forever and ever.

He promises, "I will never leave you nor forsake you" (Hebrews 13:5 NKJV). He is not going to be with you all your life only to abandon you when you die. The Spirit of Jesus dwells in your heart, and in that day God will claim you as His very own child and take you to heaven.

God, all others will fail me at some point, but You will go
with me even to death and will escort me into heaven
to live with You through eternity. Thank You for Your
faithfulness and love that will never fail. Amen.

Carried Away by Angels

The beggar died, and was carried by
the angels into Abraham's bosom.
LUKE 16:22 KJV

When they are about to die, some Christians become radiant with joy and expectation, as if already tinged with the glories of heaven. Some even speak of angels gathering in the room, telling them that it is time to go. So they depart this life with great peace, knowing exactly where they are headed.

Other Christians, while they believe in Jesus, face death with a measure of anxiety and even fear. They don't report seeing angels. So are they not going to paradise?

The answer is that not all people are given a glimpse of the magnificent heavenly dimension before departing this life. Nevertheless, angels come to take all believers home. "And he will send out his angels. . .and they will gather his chosen ones" (Matthew 24:31 NLT).

After describing the sure hope of Jesus returning in the rapture to gather believers to Himself, Paul concludes, "Comfort one another with these words" (1 Thessalonians 4:18 KJV). God's promises give great assurance and comfort that we can trust Him to take us to heaven.

Father, I know that Your Word tells me that when I die,
I will go to heaven. Yet sometimes I feel anxious when I
think about it. Give me Your peace and help me to see
death as a transition into eternity with You. Amen.

Failure

Success or Failure

They refused to trust him. So he ended their lives in failure.
PSALM 78:32–33 NLT

Worldly people refuse to trust God, yet for years they may experience "success." However, as their life comes to a close, the glitter of material possessions and accolades fades, leaving them feeling empty. And in the end, they die, taking nothing with them into eternity.

Although the world may have considered them a success, in God's eyes they failed. "For what shall it profit a man, if he shall gain the whole world, and lose his own soul?" (Mark 8:36 KJV).

Even as a Christian, if you focus inordinately on material things and give little priority to spiritual matters, you will end your days in failure. Neglect the Lord and you will experience a sense of futility. You will still be saved but will reach the end of your life having missed much of what the Lord had planned for you.

How much better to make time for reading scripture, praying, and serving God and others, then arrive in heaven to hear Jesus say, "Well done, good and faithful servant. . . . Enter into the joy of your lord" (Matthew 25:21 NKJV).

Lord, help me to see success through Your eyes, not the world's. I want to pursue Your will and not chase after earthly wealth and fame, which is futile. I want to hear You say, "Well done" at the end of my life. That is true success. Amen.

Feeling Like a Failure

"I have labored in vain, I have spent
my strength for nothing and in vain."
ISAIAH 49:4 NKJV

Some people, as they approach the end of their lives, sigh contentedly that they have no regrets. How different it is for others: they have many regrets! They may feel that most of their life was a failure, especially if they squandered years on alcohol or failed in marriage or as a parent. Or if their biggest accomplishment was to hold down a nine-to-five job and they never did anything outstanding, they may feel as if they accomplished little.

Many Christians could certainly do more for the Lord. However, many people are also too hard on themselves. Even after a lifetime of being faithful to God and their family, they lament, "I have labored in vain." But they can also say with the last part of the verse, "Yet surely my just reward is with the LORD, and my work with my God" (Isaiah 49:4 NKJV).

God sees your faithfulness. You may feel like you have failed, but He says, "I have called him. I will bring him, and he will succeed in his mission" (Isaiah 48:15 NIV).

Father, sometimes I feel like a failure, but You said You
have plans for me, good plans. They may seem small to
the world, but You promised that Your plans will succeed
and You will reward those who are faithful. Amen.

Doomed to Failure

"Why are you disobeying the LORD's command? This will not succeed!"
NUMBERS 14:41 NIV

Disobeying God guarantees failure—if not immediately, then in due time. When you ignore His laws, you set yourself up for a fall. It's the same if you jump off a building: you will suffer the painful consequences because the law of gravity always works.

In the same way, you can't violate God's spiritual laws and prosper. They too have consequences. After the Israelites refused to go into the Promised Land, God commanded them to wander in the wilderness. *Then* they decided to invade Canaan, but it was too late. God was no longer with them. Moses warned, "This will not succeed!" Sure enough, they suffered a stinging defeat.

Many people live in failure because they refuse to obey God's laws. Even many Christians live defeated lives, spinning their wheels but accomplishing little of lasting value because they are not obeying God.

You can avoid failure by loving God and following His Word. Ask Him to show you what to do every day. Then do it. "Thank God! He gives us victory. . .through our Lord Jesus Christ" (1 Corinthians 15:57 NLT).

Holy Spirit, help me to know when I am out of Your will. Show me what You want me to do, because I want the victory that only comes through obedience to Your will and will glorify Your name. Amen.

Fruit of Your Labor

*Strangers will consume your wealth, and someone
else will enjoy the fruit of your labor.*
PROVERBS 5:10 NLT

The Bible commands God's people to avoid sexual sin and states one of the penalties for breaking this rule: "someone else will enjoy the fruit of your labor." Yet some people won't listen, and Solomon describes them later lamenting, "If only I had not ignored all the warnings! . . . I have come to the brink of utter ruin" (Proverbs 5:12, 14 NLT).

People also crash and burn through reckless or dishonest financial practices. If they break those rules, many months or years of hard work can come crashing down. Failing simply because things didn't turn out as you'd hoped after doing your best is one thing. Setting yourself up for failure by cheating or cutting corners is quite another.

God wants to spare you from failure in *every* area of life. His desire is to see you rewarded for all your years of hard work. He wants to see you, not some stranger, enjoy the fruit of your labor. So stay close to Him and obey Him, and you will achieve success.

---

*Father, help me to walk in the right path of obedience so
that I can enjoy the fruit of my labor. Don't let me waste
precious time and energy following futile pursuits that
will end in failure. I want to be in Your will. Amen.*

Family Feuds
Resolving Divisions

They had such a sharp disagreement that they parted company.
ACTS 15:39 NIV

Paul was the inspired apostle who wrote 1 Corinthians 13, the beautiful "love chapter." For his part, Barnabas "was a good man, full of the Holy Spirit" (Acts 11:24 NKJV), constantly encouraging others (v. 23). You would think that they would get along—and for years they did. But one day they had such a heated argument that they could no longer work together.

It began when they were heading out on their second missionary trip. Barnabas wanted to take his cousin Mark, but Paul was set against it since Mark had deserted them previously. Both men were filled with God's Spirit, but they were also strong-willed and opinionated.

Similar scenarios often replay in today's churches and Christian families. Minor disagreements harden into ill will, with both sides unwilling to humble themselves and take the necessary steps to make amends. This can develop into a major family feud.

However, nursing hard feelings isn't God's way. He longs for love, peace, and reconciliation. Fortunately, Paul, Barnabas, and Mark forgave one another and later worked together again (1 Corinthians 9:6; Colossians 4:10).

Lord, I don't want to allow arguments to turn family members into enemies. Show me how to reconcile with my family without going against my principles or Your Word so that I can honor the relationships and glorify Your name. Amen.

Blended Families

"You are not going to get any inheritance in our family,"
they said, "because you are the son of another woman."

JUDGES 11:2 NIV

Jephthah's half brothers rejected him because his mother was a prostitute whom their father had slept with. As long as their father was alive, they were obliged to tolerate Jephthah. But as soon as their father died, the brothers kicked Jephthah out of the house, informing him that they had never accepted him as family.

That had to hurt. While such heavy-handed violence is thankfully rare, this kind of rejection is not uncommon. Thank God for blended families who live in harmony, but at times stepsiblings have difficulty accepting one another. Often this is because parents show favoritism to their natural children and the stepsiblings resent this. Even biological brothers and sisters quarrel and fight, but they may be more inclined to make amends with one another.

If you have God's love in your heart, He will help you overcome such divisions and differences. His Word says, "Sympathize with each other. Love each other as brothers and sisters. Be tenderhearted" (1 Peter 3:8 NLT).

Father, help me to live in peace and harmony within my family.
Sometimes disagreements arise between family members, so show
me how to sympathize with others and make amends when those
disagreements arise so that peace reigns in our family. Amen.

Sibling Rivalry

David's oldest brother. . .burned with anger at him. . . .
"Now what have I done?" said David.
1 SAMUEL 17:28–29 NIV

Eliab, Jesse's oldest son, had a commanding presence (1 Samuel 16:6–7). He was aware of his good looks and, as the eldest, demanded respect. But God had bypassed Eliab and his brothers to pick David, the youngest. Sibling rivalry was definitely at play.

Jesse had sent David to the battle lines, but Eliab didn't know that, so he angrily asked, "Why have you come down here? . . . I know how conceited you are and how wicked your heart is; you came down only to watch the battle" (1 Samuel 17:28 NIV). "Now what have I done?" David asked. He was apparently used to Eliab verbally attacking him.

You may have a sharp-tongued brother or sister who is quick to misjudge you and is constantly ascribing wrong motives to you. Your sibling may be jealous, or perhaps you had a run-in years earlier and he or she has never gotten over it.

Whatever your sibling may do, refuse to answer tit for tat. Rise above sibling rivalry, be at peace with your family, and seek to restore broken relationships.

Holy Spirit, help me to rise above petty offenses that happen
in life and avoid the temptation to engage in arguments
within my family. Help me to be a peacemaker so that we
can live at peace with each other and with You. Amen.

Avoid Troublemakers

God hates. . .a troublemaker in the family.
PROVERBS 6:16, 19 MSG

Some people have a permanent negative attitude and try to make others miserable with their constant criticism, quickness to take offense, and continual complaining. Or they spread gossip, creating animosity and suspicion. Perhaps there is someone like that in your extended family.

In Proverbs 6, Solomon lists seven things God particularly dislikes, and number seven is "a troublemaker in the family." The New Living Translation has "a person who sows discord in a family." The New International Version has "a person who stirs up conflict." So having a troublemaker in the family was a common problem even back then.

Proverbs 22:10 (NKJV) says, "Cast out the scoffer, and contention will leave; yes, strife. . .will cease." You can't cast an unpleasant person out of the family, but the takeaway here is that you can avoid spending time in that person's company.

If you must invite a family troublemaker to a get-together, be aware of where she is, and don't take her comments to heart. Let her negativity roll like water off a duck's back, and pray that God will either change her or limit the damage she does.

Father, I lift to You those in my family who like to make trouble,
and I pray You would be at work in their spirits and lives.
Be at work in my spirit to maintain love and peace toward
them because I can only do that in Your strength. Amen.

Family Stress

Doing Your Fair Share

*"Lord, do You not care that my sister has left me
to serve alone? Therefore tell her to help me."*

LUKE 10:40 NKJV

Martha was "worried and troubled about many things" (Luke 10:41
NKJV). Jesus, Israel's Messiah, was visiting, and she wanted to present
a splendid feast. They were likely a wealthy family and may have
had servants. If so, Martha could have left the cooking and serving
to them, but she insisted on micromanaging preparations.

Her sister Mary, however, had chosen to listen to Jesus. After
all, Israel's Messiah was visiting, and she wanted to make the most
of the opportunity. Jesus commended Mary and refused to send her
into the kitchen.

Most modern homes don't have servants, so the right thing to
do is to get up and help do the work that needs to be done. If not,
one person ends up doing it all—whether cleaning, cooking, dishes,
or whatever. And if this becomes a regular pattern, it creates stress
in the home.

In a family, every member needs to carry his or her share of
the load. Even children should have regular duties and fulfill them.

---

*God, give me the spirit of a helper and help me not to let my
temper get the better of me when it seems like others aren't
doing their fair share. I don't want to stress over mundane
tasks but rather do my part without grumbling. Amen.*

Feeling Unappreciated

*"You have made them equal to us who
have borne the burden of the work."*
MATTHEW 20:12 NIV

When the prodigal son staggered home, filthy and starving, his father threw a feast. His other son complained, "I've stayed here serving you, never giving you one moment of grief, but have you ever thrown a party for me and my friends? Then this son of yours. . .shows up and you go all out with a feast!" (Luke 15:29–30 MSG). It didn't seem fair.

Because the older brother had worked hard every day and tried his best to please his father, he felt unappreciated when his father threw a party for his prodigal brother. Actually, the father was simply celebrating seeing a son whom he had feared dead. Likewise, modern children sometimes misread their parents' motives.

When one of your children is struggling, you may show them extra attention, but although your motives are good, be aware how things might look to your other children, and explain that you deeply appreciate them and all they do.

"We are taking pains to do what is right, not only in the eyes of the Lord but also in the eyes of man" (2 Corinthians 8:21 NIV).

---

*Father, help me to be aware of my actions so that I don't
show preferential treatment. If one family member needs
extra help, show me how to do it in a way that the rest
of the family feels loved and appreciated. Amen.*

Caring for Your Family

Anyone who neglects to care for family
members in need repudiates the faith.
1 Timothy 5:8 msg

The Bible says that a strong proof that your faith is genuine is if you love other Christians (John 13:35). It also says that even if you say you love God, you are lying if you hate other believers (1 John 4:20). And you are expected to prove your love in practical ways by sharing food and clothing with them if they are in need (1 John 3:16–18).

It should come as no surprise, therefore, that God considers love for your immediate family to be definitive proof of your faith. And He expects you to demonstrate love by caring, tangible actions.

Your primary duty as mothers and fathers is to provide food, clothing, and shelter for your children; to meet their medical and dental needs; and to spend time with them, nurturing them. If you are divorced, be faithful with child support. Don't look on it as a burden, but provide cheerfully.

Much needless stress is caused when parents fail to grasp the importance of these basic responsibilities. But obeying this principle is obeying the heart of Jesus' message.

Lord, my family should come second to only You. Show me
any time that I am neglecting them in any way. Show me
where they need help and how I can be there for them so
that they know they are loved and cared for. Amen.

Meeting Expectations

Fathers, do not exasperate your children; instead,
bring them up in the training and instruction of the Lord.
EPHESIANS 6:4 NIV

Paul instructed fathers not to exasperate their children. Most parents, however, feel that their children's behavior is more likely to exasperate them. You try to train them to do the right things, but they often stubbornly resist, complain, fight with their brothers and sisters, and make you unhappy. This creates ongoing stress in the home and is liable to produce short tempers.

Here is where you have to have faith that a loving approach, constant instruction, and consistent training will eventually have an effect, transform your children from the inside out, and round off their rough edges.

If you lose faith in the gentle approach, you may try sledgehammer tactics, barking out commands and forcing your child to obey. That may well produce immediate outward results, but it won't work in the long run. . .and it will exasperate your children.

How much better to involve your child in the process! It may take longer for their behavior to change and for them to meet your expectations, but the change will be genuine and lasting.

Father, help me to be consistent in training and disciplining my
children with love and patience. Give me the strength to endure
through difficult times, knowing that You are at work in their
lives and that the result will be well worth the wait. Amen.

Fragmented Families

All the others care only for themselves and
not for what matters to Jesus Christ.
PHILIPPIANS 2:21 NLT

For thousands of years, one of the defining traits of a family was that individual members cared for each other, pulled together, and did their share to make things work. The following verse about the church also holds true for a healthy family: "There should be no schism in the body, but. . .members should have the same care for one another" (1 Corinthians 12:25 NKJV).

Unfortunately, this is not the case in many modern families. Many families are divided and fragmented. Often parents and brothers and sisters live in the same house but "care only for themselves."

Christians proclaim their love and faith in God, but if they focus on what matters to Jesus, they realize the importance of loving their fellow humans, beginning with their own family members. "He has given us this command: Anyone who loves God must also love their brother and sister" (1 John 4:21 NIV).

Yes, people these days are busy, and they have their own interests. This is understandable. But they need to interact in love and help one another as a family.

Lord, I don't want my family to be fragmented. How can
I better interact with them to show my love and promote
healing and reconciliation? I'm asking You to restore my
family to wholeness as only You can do. Amen.

Fear

I Shall Not Fear

Whenever I am afraid, I will trust in You.
PSALM 56:3 NKJV

King David had many enemies and was constantly fighting battles against them. He admitted that he felt fear at times, but he had also learned from experience what to do in such situations. Rather than give in to his fear and run, he cried out to the Lord.

David said to God, "Whenever I am afraid, I will trust in You" (Psalm 56:3 NKJV). You notice that David didn't say, "*If* I am afraid"— as if he was so brave that it was highly unlikely he would experience fear. He said, "*Whenever* I am afraid" (emphasis added). He too knew fear. But he also knew how to deal with it: he trusted God.

Trusting in God means you believe that God will protect you. This is why David also said, "Though I walk through the valley of the shadow of death, I will fear no evil; for You are with me" (Psalm 23:4 NKJV). Fear is a very common human emotion, and that is why the Bible has so much to say about it and tells us so often how to overcome it.

God, like David I want to trust You when I am afraid.
I know that no matter what happens, You are with me.
Help me to overcome my fear and have the victory only
You can give as I face today's battles. Amen.

Unshaken by Bad News

*They do not fear bad news; they confidently
trust the LORD to care for them.*

PSALM 112:7 NLT

Psalm 112 opens by saying, "How joyful are those who fear the LORD
and delight in obeying his commands" (v. 1 NLT). These are the people
whom verse 7 (NLT) refers to, saying, "They do not fear bad news;
they confidently trust the LORD to care for them."

King Ahaz, however, is an example of someone who didn't
love or trust God. When he heard news that his two worst enemies
were conspiring to invade his land, "the hearts of Ahaz and his
people were shaken, as the trees of the forest are shaken by the
wind" (Isaiah 7:2 NIV).

If you are constantly in the habit of looking to God, it is much
easier for you to trust Him when trouble comes. For one thing, if you
know you are doing your best to obey Him, you have more assurance
that He will answer your prayers. "God does not hear sinners; but
if anyone is a worshiper of God and does His will, He hears him"
(John 9:31 NKJV).

Confidently trust in God. He is looking out for you.

---

*Father, I want to be unshakeable no matter what the
day brings. The world is full of bad news, and tribulations
are sure to come, but help me to confidently trust in You
to handle every situation and to fear not. Amen.*

Overcoming Fear

*"You will live in such fear that the sound of a
leaf driven by the wind will send you fleeing."*
LEVITICUS 26:36 NLT

God warned that if His people disobeyed Him, "I will make their hearts so fearful. . .that the sound of a windblown leaf will put them to flight. They will run. . .and they will fall, even though no one is pursuing them" (Leviticus 26:36 NIV). Today we call this paranoia.

God doesn't desire His children to live in fear, but people bring fear on themselves through disobedience. "God hath not given us the spirit of fear; but of power, and of love, and of a sound mind" (2 Timothy 1:7 KJV).

When you depart from God, your protection vanishes and your fears begin to close in on you. Soon you complain, "The thing which I greatly feared is come upon me" (Job 3:25 KJV). Then you are running from your own shadow—or a scuttling leaf.

If you are plagued by fear, repent of any sin in your heart. Then trust God to forgive you, and He will. He promised in His Word that He would (1 John 1:8–9).

---

*Lord, if there is any disobedience in me, please show me
and forgive me. Lead me in the way that I should go,
because I want to live in obedience to Your will so that
I have no need to fear what lies ahead. Amen.*

Be of Good Courage

*Be strong and of a good courage, fear not, nor be afraid of
them: for the LORD. . .will not fail thee, nor forsake thee.*
DEUTERONOMY 31:6 KJV

Fear is a tremendously debilitating thing. It can suck the life right out
of you. It can make you throw up your hands in defeat before the fight
even begins. And if you were in this by yourself, that might be a logical
thing to do. After all, why face an enemy who vastly outguns you?

But there is a good reason to have courage: the Lord is on your
side. He won't cave in when you need Him most; He won't suddenly
realize that He is not strong enough; nor will He abandon you in your
crisis. These are very encouraging thoughts.

The enemy will try to overwhelm you with feelings of apprehension, but remind yourself of who is on your side and face down your
fear. Don't blink, and even if you are hit with a wave of fear, stand
your ground. That wave is merely a tactic of the enemy and will crash
harmlessly against the great rock on which you have taken refuge.

---

*God, with You on my side I have no reason to fear. You are
greater than any enemy I face, so I will trust in You. You have
already overcome the world, and victory is mine because
You said You will never forsake me nor fail me. Amen.*

Financial Strain

Waiting for Economic Recovery

*"All this misery is from the LORD! Why should
I wait for the LORD any longer?"*

2 KINGS 6:33 NLT

In the days of King Jehoram of Israel, the Syrians had besieged Samaria, and the siege lasted so long that there was a great famine: a donkey's head was sold for eighty shekels ($1,120), and one cup of dove's dung sold for five shekels ($70) (2 Kings 6:25 KJV).

Elisha had been advising the king to trust God, but finally the king snapped, stormed up to Elisha's door, and shouted, "All this misery is from the LORD! Why should I wait for the LORD any longer?"

Your faith can be tested to the limit when you wait and wait for a financial breakthrough, to the point where you are tempted to abandon hope. You may conclude that God is against you and is, in fact, the one causing your problems. So you lash out at those who encourage you to hope. Yet in the Israelites' case, the next day God did a miracle and provided enough food for everyone (see 2 Kings 7:1–16).

God can still do miracles today. Don't abandon hope.

---

*Father, I am facing a financial crisis, and it seems hopeless. I know
that You are able to do miracles, and I really need a miracle right
now. Even so, I will trust and hope in You in the meantime. Amen.*

Soaring Food Costs

"A loaf of wheat bread or three loaves
of barley will cost a day's pay."
REVELATION 6:6 NLT

During times of war, natural disaster, or drought, the price of food has always risen—and the Bible warns that during the closing chapter of earth's history, prices will rise to astronomical levels.

Food prices have already increased dramatically in recent years. One of the main reasons is that farm machinery consumes much fuel, as do the trucks that transport food. Also, major aquifers that farmers have depended on for decades are running dry. In addition, year after year of no rainfall in major food-producing regions is causing prices to spike.

All of these factors have put a constant financial strain on families, who must now allocate a greater portion of their monthly budget to food.

The short-term solution is to find ways to earn a little extra cash, learn to budget better, and do without nonessentials. But the only solution to the final tribulation and food crisis is for God to bring paradise down to earth, creating justice and plenty for all. As Christians, we earnestly wait for that day.

Lord, help me to be wise and plan well during hard times,
but I know You are my provider. Show me how to trust
that You'll take care of me, even when the world is in
chaos, and to wait patiently for Your return. Amen.

Uncertain Finances

Take no thought for your life, what ye
shall eat, or what ye shall drink.
MATTHEW 6:25 KJV

Many Christians consider the phrase "Take no thought for your life" to be impractical advice. How can you help but take constant thought for your life? You need to stay on top of every detail of your work and home life to make sure things get done.

But a more accurate translation is, "Take no *anxious thought* for your life." This is why both the NIV and the NKJV translate this phrase, "Do not worry about your life."

You may have a steady nine-to-five job that holds no surprises and supplies a guaranteed paycheck. Although you find your work somewhat boring, you don't worry much. But Christ's admonition is especially comforting when you run your own business, are self-employed, or work on commission, and your finances alternate between feast and famine.

And in difficult financial times, with employment more insecure and steadily rising prices, you need the reassurance that God will supply all your needs. He has promised to do just that (see Philippians 4:19). So don't worry.

I will not be anxious, God, because You promise to supply all my needs
regardless of my circumstances or my finances. Help me not to worry
but to keep my eyes on You and be obedient to Your will. Amen.

Running Up Debt

It's stupid to try to get something for nothing,
or run up huge bills you can never pay.
PROVERBS 17:18 MSG

Contrary to the Bible's warnings, many Christians hope to benefit from monetary windfalls without doing any work. They daydream of winning the lottery and enjoying a life of ease.

It's just as irresponsible to constantly pull out their credit card and run up huge bills with no idea how they will be able to pay them. They may be hoping that God will bless them with huge finances out of left field, but that is not the way God made His world to work.

God's basic financial plan hasn't changed in thousands of years: "Whoever gathers money little by little makes it grow," and "Hard work brings a profit, but mere talk leads only to poverty" (Proverbs 13:11; 14:23 NIV).

Of course, when starting up a new business, you often must borrow money to launch out. There are times when you need to take calculated financial risks—with the emphasis on "calculated." You should have a well-thought-out plan on how you will repay the money. Do that and you will avoid much financial stress.

Lord, help me to be responsible with what You have given me
and not to overuse credit cards or run up bills that I can't afford
in order to buy things that will not last. Help me to be a hard
worker for You and appreciate what I do have. Amen.

Giving Wisely

I do not mean that others should be eased and you burdened.
2 Corinthians 8:13 nkjv

When Paul was writing to the Corinthians about giving money to help the impoverished Christians in Jerusalem, he assured them that God would bless them for giving generously but didn't want them donating so much that they themselves ended up financially short.

You are required to give to God, and many Christians believe in tithing 10 percent of their income. But some churches also encourage people to give "freewill offerings" above and beyond that. A few, quoting Mark 12:41–44, pressure you to "sacrificially" give money you have allocated for food and rent. This can leave you under intense financial strain.

If you can afford to give and feel you should, by all means do. But avoid being pressured to give if you don't have it to spare. You may be asked to donate to a truly worthy cause, but your first responsibility is to care for your family.

God blesses generous giving, but He also gives you wisdom to help you avoid spending money you shouldn't spend or giving money you shouldn't give and thereby bringing hardship on yourself.

Holy Spirit, guide me as I try to give with a generous heart and open hands, but help me to know Your will so that I give wisely. Show me when to give sacrificially and when to say no to requests that will cause hardship for my family. Amen.

Foreclosure/Eviction

Losing Your Home

Even now we go hungry and thirsty. . .and have no home.
1 CORINTHIANS 4:11 NLT

It's devastating to be uprooted and lose your home. But if you can no longer afford to pay your mortgage, you have no choice but to give up your house. Then you may be forced to move from one cheap rental to another.

Jesus didn't have a home either. After His life's work began, He was constantly on the road. He said, "Foxes have dens to live in, and birds have nests, but the Son of Man has no place even to lay his head" (Matthew 8:20 NLT). He gave up His home to travel around sharing the gospel.

Paul didn't have a home either. He had "no certain dwellingplace" (1 Corinthians 4:11 KJV). He was constantly moving from place to place, never sure where he would sleep next. But he accepted this and said, "If we have food and clothing, we will be content with that" (1 Timothy 6:8 NIV).

If you are discouraged about losing your house, remember: this world is not your promised home. God is preparing a mansion in heaven for you.

Father, I am grateful for what I do have, but I am also discouraged about my circumstances. Help me to keep my focus on You and trust in Your plan for my life, even when it is not what I had hoped for. Amen.

Driven from Home

They were forced to live in the dry stream beds,
among the rocks and in holes in the ground.

JOB 30:6 NIV

Bible lands often had turbulent histories, with invading armies sweeping across the landscape or civil wars causing upheavals. People were forced from their homes and took shelter wherever they could. "They wandered in the wilderness. . .; they found no city to dwell in" (Psalm 107:4 KJV).

This scenario is being repeated in war-torn nations today. Christians in countries such as Syria and Iraq have had to flee their homes on short notice or be executed.

We can be thankful for the peace we enjoy. Still, these are troubled times, and many people in our nation are forced out of their homes through foreclosure. Being uprooted from your home of many years can be a traumatic experience.

Even though you know that some people have troubles much worse than yours, that doesn't invalidate your suffering. God sympathizes with your pain too. And your sorrow gives you greater empathy for the suffering of others. It also gives you good reason to be thankful when you find a secure place once again.

God, thank You for the peace I enjoy at the moment, but I also
know that circumstances can change at any moment. Help me
to be sympathetic to those who are going through the trauma
of losing their home and to help as You see fit. Amen.

Thrust from the Nest

The women of Moab are left like homeless birds.
ISAIAH 16:2 NLT

In Isaiah's day, the Assyrians were invading Judah—as well as Moab to the east. Isaiah described a situation where the men of Moab had been defeated in battle and the women and children were fleeing their towns ahead of the advancing armies.

The New International Version describes them "like fluttering birds pushed from the nest" (Isaiah 16:2 NIV). If you have ever seen a baby bird fluttering frantically and helplessly, you get an idea of the panic and loss these women were experiencing.

Perhaps you can identify. You can if you are being evicted from your home—either because you can no longer pay your mortgage or are behind on your rent. Not knowing where you will move to can be overwhelming. Like Abraham, you head out, not knowing where you are going (Hebrews 11:8).

But God promised the wandering Israelites, "I am sending an angel ahead of you to guard you along the way and to bring you to the place I have prepared" (Exodus 23:20 NIV). May this promise be a comfort to you as well.

Father, sometimes I don't like the path ahead, but if You are leading me, then You go before me, preparing the way. Help me to trust You more and follow You without fear even when the path seems hard. Amen.

Helplessness

You Are Not Helpless

I can do everything through Christ, who gives me strength.
PHILIPPIANS 4:13 NLT

At times you will be overwhelmed by problems and circumstances, and it can be frightening to be swept along by situations that seem to be completely beyond your control.

But although you are powerless to deal with insurmountable problems, you are never completely helpless, because the all-powerful God is with you. Christ lives in you, and He can strengthen you and give you solutions and just the right answers.

The armies of Israel felt helpless against Goliath, but David, emboldened by the Spirit of God, faced the giant and defeated him. Paul tells us, "Be strong in the Lord, and in the power of his might" (Ephesians 6:10 KJV).

Do you feel weak and helpless? Rejoice! This gives God the opportunity to work miracles through you. As Paul wrote, "When I am weak, then am I strong" (2 Corinthians 12:10 KJV). God assured him, "My strength is made perfect in weakness" (2 Corinthians 12:9 KJV).

Even when things are darkest, you can always pray. God can do the impossible, and with Him on your side, things are never completely out of control.

Lord, I am weak and helpless without You, but I know that with You I can do hard things in Your strength. The path ahead seems dark and impossible to bear, but with You I know all things are possible. Amen.

The Hopes of the Helpless

Lord, you know the hopes of the helpless.
Surely you will hear their cries and comfort them.
PSALM 10:17 NLT

Many people today are helpless. They are boxed into desperate situations over which they have no control. Their only recourse is to cry out to God.

This applies to families trying to make ends meet on a limited budget—only to be hit by a large, unexpected expense. It applies to single mothers trying to raise children in a difficult part of town. It applies to seniors struggling with health issues. God knows each of their sorrows and needs, and He hears their cries for help.

Usually, however, God doesn't do outstanding miracles and completely transform their situations. Instead, He answers incrementally, day by day, in almost imperceptible ways, helping them manage through desperate times and comforting them in their sorrow. "Blessed be God. . .the Father of mercies, and the God of all comfort" (2 Corinthians 1:3 KJV).

God knows the hopes of the helpless, His heart is moved by their pain, and He acts to bring them relief, even when it seems that He is not present.

Father, my situation seems hopeless, but Your Word says that You hear my prayers even when I can't see You at work, so I will trust in You. You are the God of all comfort. Blessed be Your name. Amen.

Utterly Helpless

"I am utterly helpless, without any chance of success."

JOB 6:13 NLT

After losing all his earthly belongings—and even his family—in a series of calamities, and after months of suffering painful boils all over his body, Job was ready to call it quits. He lamented, "I have nothing to live for" (Job 6:11 NLT). He had been completely beaten down.

Job was convinced that no matter what he attempted, he would fail. He had absolutely zero chance of succeeding in anything he tried to do. So why even bother?

Sometimes you may feel that way. Life has dealt you hard blows, and just when you are struggling to get back on your feet, you are knocked down again. It seems as if God has conspired against you, or even if He hasn't, He still isn't with you while life puts you through the wringer.

But God was always there with Job and had never abandoned him—even if it looked as if He had. God just had to take Job through a particularly difficult season of life, and once that was over, He restored Job's riches and caused him to succeed again. He will do the same for you.

Lord, it seems like there is no hope for me, and I am utterly helpless, but difficult seasons come to everyone. Help me to trust You even when I can't see You at work, because seasons come but they also go, and good times will return again. Amen.

God Sees the Helpless

The LORD replies, "I have seen violence done to the helpless."
PSALM 12:5 NLT

Sometimes you wonder if God actually sees how the wicked oppress the helpless—and if He sees, if He cares—because the wicked keep on hurting the weak. But in the verse above (NLT), God goes on to say, "Now I will rise up to rescue them, as they have longed for me to do."

You may be suffering oppression from someone who has great power, and there is nobody to deliver you out of that person's hand. You may wonder how long it will take for the Lord to act.

God often takes His time, but His delays don't mean that He overlooks the wrong that was done, or *is* being done. He doesn't. And though you may be unable to alter the outcome, God is far from helpless. He is all-powerful, and what is more, He is a just God and cares for you. So He will act.

But He doesn't settle every score and right every wrong in this life. Many He reserves for the day of judgment when the righteous will be rewarded and the unjust will be condemned (see 2 Thessalonians 1:4–10; James 5:1–9).

---

*Father, sometimes it seems like You don't care, but I know
You see my situation. Your ways are not my ways, so teach
me how to be patient and to wait on Your timing because
You will reward the faithful in due time. Amen.*

Weakness Transformed

*Their weakness was turned to strength. They became
strong in battle and put whole armies to flight.*
HEBREWS 11:34 NLT

Hebrews 11:32 mentions Gideon as one of the heroes who accomplished great things. But Gideon started off weak. He protested to the angel of the Lord, "How can I rescue Israel? My clan is the weakest in the whole tribe of Manasseh, and I am the least in my entire family!" (Judges 6:15 NLT).

Nevertheless, Gideon believed God and gathered an army to fight the Midianites and Amalekites. And because he believed, God made him strong in battle and he put the invading armies to flight.

God often chooses weak, helpless people to accomplish His purposes. He could choose strong people—and sometimes does—but then they tend to get the idea that they were victorious *because* they were strong. But if they know they are weak, they realize they overcame only because God helped them.

You may feel weak and incapable, completely overwhelmed by your circumstances. But if you pray desperately, God can transform your weakness into strength and empower you to do amazing things.

---

*Lord, I am weak, but You are strong and mighty. I can do nothing
on my own, but You transform weakness into strength when I
am obedient to Your will. So, use me to accomplish Your will
through Your might so that You may be glorified. Amen.*

Hidden Sin

God Searches Your Heart

Search me, O God, and know my heart: try me, and know my thoughts: and see if there be any wicked way in me.

PSALM 139:23–24 KJV

All Christians sin from time to time. But God is more than willing to forgive: "If we say that we have no sin, we deceive ourselves. . . . If we confess our sins, he is faithful and just to forgive us our sins, and to cleanse us from all unrighteousness" (1 John 1:8–9 KJV).

However, the problem comes when believers don't seek to make things right. Sometimes you don't recognize that you have done wrong, or—as is often the case—you are aware that you have sinned but aren't ready to repent. Or you don't take your sin seriously. You tell yourself that you are only human, and it is a trifling matter, after all.

But sin causes a disconnect in your relationship with God, so it is wise to pray, "Search me, O God," then listen carefully to what He brings to your attention. If you want to walk in the light, you must continually surrender any darkness in your life to God.

God, search my heart and try me. Show me where I have sinned. Please forgive me and help me to walk in Your light so that I can live a life that glorifies You. Let this be my daily prayer. Amen.

Covering Sin

He who covers his sins will not prosper, but whoever
confesses and forsakes them will have mercy.
PROVERBS 28:13 NKJV

Sometimes believers struggle with hidden sin. They are in agony over something they have done but are scared to bring it to the light. The reason is shame or fear: they worry about their reputations. What would people think if they knew they had done such a selfish thing? *No,* they reason, *better to keep it covered.* So they continue to suffer—and to miss out on the blessings God longs to give them—because "he who covers his sins will not prosper."

There is wisdom in not describing a private sin (something that concerns only the sinner and God) publicly. Since so many people love gossip, the sinner would only open himself to needless pain. Also, if he has offended someone, the Bible says that the ideal solution is to go to that person alone and apologize (Matthew 18:15).

Confessing certain personal faults to mature spiritual friends is also appropriate at times. "Confess your faults one to another, and pray one for another, that ye may be healed" (James 5:16 KJV). God longs to give you both wisdom and peace.

Lord, I know I have sinned. Please forgive me and show me how
to make it right, because I want a clear conscience and a right
relationship with You. Thank You for Your grace and mercy.
Help me to be transparent before You and others. Amen.

Achan's Stolen Treasure

"I coveted them and took them. They are
hidden in the ground inside my tent."
Joshua 7:21 niv

An Israelite named Achan disobeyed God's command not to take any of Jericho's treasure, and he buried choice items inside his tent. Consequently, God judged the entire nation, causing the Israelites to suffer their first defeat in battle.

So often the innocent suffer because of the guilty. And like Achan, the guilty cover up what they have done and never confess it. Perhaps you work for a business where items have gone missing and everyone is under suspicion and being penalized for one person's actions.

Or perhaps you were careless or negligent, and because you didn't own up to it right away when the situation still could have been salvaged, you caused your company a major loss. It's an awful feeling to be on the outs with everyone over something you now would have done differently.

The best thing you can do is learn from your lesson and make sure never to repeat it. "He will speak peace to His people. . . ; but let them not turn back to folly" (Psalm 85:8 nkjv).

God, I have made mistakes. Help me to learn from them, and show
me how to make amends to those who were affected by my actions.
Most of all, help me not to repeat my mistakes in the future. Amen.

Hopelessness

God Never Disregards You

Why do you complain, Jacob? Why do you say, Israel, "My way is hidden from the LORD; my cause is disregarded by my God"?

ISAIAH 40:27 NIV

Hope, along with love and faith, is a key virtue (1 Corinthians 13:13). To lose hope leaves a great gnawing emptiness inside you. Though you still believe in God, if you lose hope that He loves you and think that He has turned His face away, you are basically just a shell of yourself.

Imagine being convinced that God cares so little about you that He completely ignores you. He is aware that you are mired in problems, but He simply can't be bothered to help you or comfort you. Talk about hopelessness!

The truth is very different. God loves you, and your cause is constantly before His eyes. He made certain of that by permanently etching your name on His hands. He says, "Can a mother forget the baby at her breast. . . ? Though she may forget, I will not forget you! See, I have engraved you on the palms of my hands" (Isaiah 49:15–16 NIV).

God sees what you are going through, and He cares immensely.

Father, my name is engraved upon Your palm, so I know You see me and care for me. Even when I feel like no one else sees me or remembers me, I know I can rely on You. Therefore, I have hope. Amen.

147

Withstanding Fear

"We're all afraid. Everyone in the country feels hopeless."
JOSHUA 2:9 MSG

When God was ready to lead the Israelites into Canaan, He struck great fear into the hearts of the Canaanites so they'd melt away before His people. The Lord did amazing miracles to convince them that it was futile to fight Him. And it worked. The harlot Rahab told the spies, "We're all afraid. Everyone in the country feels hopeless."

However, sometimes God's people experience paralyzing fear too. This often happens when they are disobeying Him in some way. God warned, "There were they in great fear, where no fear was" (Psalm 53:5 KJV). Many people today are afraid even when they are not in imminent danger. The solution is to get their hearts right with God as quickly as possible. Then the fears and delusions will melt away.

Or the problem might not be sin; perhaps they succumb to fear and think their situation is hopeless because they are not spending enough time in prayer, looking to God. Remember that He promises, "You will keep him in perfect peace, whose mind is stayed on You, because he trusts in You" (Isaiah 26:3 NKJV).

Lord, the enemy wants to distract me with fear by what is going on in the world around me, but I will keep my focus on You. You promise to always be with me, so I will not fear. I will live in Your peace. Amen.

Hopelessly Confused

Live no longer as the Gentiles do, for they are hopelessly confused.
EPHESIANS 4:17 NLT

Before you were saved, "you were separate from Christ, . . . without hope and without God in the world" (Ephesians 2:12 NIV). You were lost and condemned. You had no purpose for living. The Bible describes this, saying: "Our days on earth are like a shadow, without hope" (1 Chronicles 29:15 NIV).

But when Jesus saved you, you gained "hope as an anchor for the soul, firm and secure" (Hebrews 6:19 NIV). This renewed your way of thinking and gave you tremendous peace and joy.

But it is important to grow in your faith and to continue to forsake your old life, such as the world's take on sexual morality or its views on spiritual truth. If you fail to do this and continue to buy into the world's philosophies, their influence will grow like yeast in a lump of dough (Galatians 5:8–9) until you eventually become confused again.

That is why the Bible commands, "Stand fast therefore in the liberty by which Christ has made us free, and do not be entangled again with a yoke of bondage" (Galatians 5:1 NKJV).

Holy Spirit, I know You are with me. Give me clarity when the world tries to deceive me and confuse me. Guide me in the truth so that I can stand fast in the liberty of Christ, anchored by hope. Amen.

What's the Use?

"The verdict has already been handed down—
'Guilty!'—so what's the use of protests or appeals?"
JOB 9:28 MSG

Sometimes you may feel like Job: there is no use in complaining to God about your situation. He has already decided to punish you, and nothing you can say or do will change things. Usually this kind of hopelessness pervades your spirit when you have sinned and aren't sure if God has forgiven you.

Or it could come over you if God is convicting you about some fault or some wrong for which you have never apologized and you are unwilling to give up the habit or to make things right. Your own heart condemns you. After a while you may even forget why God is bearing down on you—and you just have a general feeling of hopelessness hanging like a cloud over your head.

Pray today and ask God to work in your heart and bring you to repentance. "If we confess our sins, He is faithful and just to forgive us our sins and to cleanse us from all unrighteousness" (1 John 1:9 NKJV). Then believe that He *has* forgiven you and move on.

God, search me and show me if there is unconfessed sin in
my heart. Forgive me and teach me how to make amends. Then,
help me to move on once I have done all I can do instead of
wallowing in guilt for something You have already forgiven. Amen.

Believing for the Impossible

"All this may seem impossible to you now. . . .
But is it impossible for me?"
ZECHARIAH 8:6 NLT

A handful of Jews had returned from captivity to Judah, but it was a long, hard journey, and few elderly people or children had come. But God promised that the streets of Jerusalem would be full of boys and girls at play and aged men and women sitting. This population explosion seemed impossible, but God said it would happen.

Sometimes God asks you too to believe the impossible. He realizes that to your limited knowledge the situation may seem hopeless, but He seeks to remind you that He is the all-powerful Creator of the heavens and the earth, and that nothing is impossible for Him.

Perhaps you have no problem with that but just don't believe that God cares enough about your circumstances to do the miracle. To this He says, "For I know the plans I have for you, . . .plans to prosper you and not to harm you, plans to give you hope and a future" (Jeremiah 29:11 NIV).

With God on your side, your situation is far from hopeless.

God, You said You had a plan for my life that seems
impossible at this moment, but with You nothing is
impossible. Grant me the faith to keep moving forward
even when the world thinks it is hopeless. Amen.

Infertility
Desperate for Children

*When Rachel saw that she wasn't having any children. . . ,
she pleaded with Jacob, "Give me children, or I'll die!"*

GENESIS 30:1 NLT

God put a natural desire in most women to have babies. They may go for years enjoying the carefree single life, with little desire to have children. Then the nesting instinct kicks in with a vengeance, and they simply *must* have children to feel complete. God designed things this way to ensure that the human race continues.

This is why Bible women who weren't able to bear children went through such tremendous trials. We see this with Sarah, and with Hannah and Elizabeth. But no woman illustrates this better than Rachel. After she had gone years without conceiving, she became so desperate that she literally felt like dying.

Many women today also struggle with infertility. Although they have tried to get pregnant and have undergone extensive fertility treatments, nothing seems to work. And attempts at adoption face major roadblocks.

But God has done miracles in the past, and He is still able today. Don't give up hope. One way or another, God can see to it that you have children.

---

*Father, You know the desires of my heart. I trust You and Your timing
to see my desires come to pass, even if it is not in the way I had
imagined. My hope is in You alone, so I will wait for You. Amen.*

Praying for a Son

If you'll. . .go into action for me by giving me a son,
I'll give him completely, unreservedly to you.

1 SAMUEL 1:11 MSG

Hannah was desperate for a son and promised the Lord that if He gave her a child, she would dedicate him completely to God. And look at the serendipitous way God worked! He desired to raise up a powerful prophet in Israel and did so through a humble woman's misery. When Hannah made a heartfelt surrender, dedicating her son utterly to God's purposes, God was able to act—and the great prophet Samuel was born!

You may not understand why God allows you to go through severe testings by keeping you from having children. But He may well have higher purposes in mind. Perhaps He prevents you from conceiving and giving birth because He wants you to adopt a wonderful child who desperately needs you to guide him or her into a high calling.

God often works in mysterious ways to bring about His will. He may lead you through the vale of tears, not because He doesn't love you, but because sometimes only such difficult paths bring about His will.

God, I don't understand why I am going through these
trials, but Your ways are not my ways, and Your thoughts
are not my thoughts. I don't have to understand, because
I trust You to work things out for my good. Amen.

Content in God

Whom have I in heaven but You? And there is
none upon earth that I desire besides You.
PSALM 73:25 NKJV

It's a natural, good thing for a woman to desire to become pregnant—even to long earnestly for a child and to pray fervently for one. But there is a danger even in desiring good things: if you become so obsessed with something that you can't be happy without it, you have exalted your desire above God.

In addition, God intends that you find your ultimate fulfillment in Him. You aren't born with this desire. It has to be *learned*. Paul said, "I have learned to be content whatever the circumstances" (Philippians 4:11 NIV).

Often Christians claim the promise: "Delight yourself also in the LORD, and He shall give you the desires of your heart" (Psalm 37:4 NKJV). They reason, "I love God, so He is obligated to give me whatever I want." But delighting yourself in the Lord means choosing God's will, *whatever* it is, even if it runs contrary to your desires. And it sometimes does.

Certainly you should present your petitions to God. But then rest them at His feet and submit to Him.

Lord, You know my desires for a child, but I desire to know
Your will and to learn to be content wherever I am. Show
me Your will, and help me to be obedient and content
even when it is not what I thought I wanted. Amen.

Insomnia

Sleep and Fear

When thou liest down, thou shalt not be afraid:
yea, thou shalt lie down, and thy sleep shall be sweet.
PROVERBS 3:24 KJV

Worry is one of the biggest hindrances to getting a good night's sleep—especially worry about finances. "The sleep of a laboring man is sweet, . . .but the abundance of the rich will not permit him to sleep" (Ecclesiastes 5:12 NKJV). The rich toss and turn, worrying about losing their wealth. They know that all too often "riches. . .make themselves wings; they fly away" (Proverbs 23:5 NKJV).

Of course, many poor people lose sleep over money too. They are not worried about dips in the stock market or a decline in the price of gold. Usually they worry about where they will get the money to pay their bills.

God's promise of sleep applies to everyone—rich and poor. The scriptures promise, "You will keep him in perfect peace, whose mind is stayed on You" (Isaiah 26:3 NKJV). Stay focused on God's love for you and keep your mind filled with promises from His Word, and He will give you peace and rest. "God gives rest to his loved ones" (Psalm 127:2 NLT).

God, You are Jehovah Jireh, my provider. My expectation
is from You and You alone. Help me to cast my cares
on You so that I can rest, knowing my needs will be met
because they are in Your caring hands. Amen.

Sleeping in Peace

I will both lie down in peace, and sleep;
for You alone, O LORD, make me dwell in safety.
PSALM 4:8 NKJV

What's your sleep like when you are under pressure, facing stress, or being threatened? You probably have difficulty sleeping. You may hardly be able to rest at all.

When David's son Absalom led an army against him, David fled across the Jordan, where he gathered his own army. David penned a short psalm before the battle, declaring his trust in God. He proclaimed: "I lie down and sleep; I wake again, because the LORD sustains me. I will not fear though tens of thousands assail me on every side" (Psalm 3:5–6 NIV).

Think of the trouble David was in! But trusting that God shielded him and wouldn't allow him to be harmed, he lay down and slept peacefully, without tossing and turning all night. This took great faith. David had to look unswervingly at God or he would have worried himself sick.

You can't stop troubled thoughts from assailing your mind, but you can resolutely resist them. And as you do, God will give you peace, and you can sleep.

Father, I will lie down and sleep in peace because I know that You are Almighty God and You are in control. Worry will only weaken me and take my peace, but faith in You brings me strength and rest. Amen.

Unable to Sleep

You don't let me sleep. I am too distressed even to pray!
PSALM 77:4 NLT

Some people, when they wake up in the night and can't get back to sleep, spend time peacefully praying. As soon as they have communed with God for a while, they return to blissful sleep. This isn't the case with other people: they wake up but are too exhausted to properly focus. They *try* to pray. . .but mostly just lie there longing for sleep.

When you are troubled, you are usually highly motivated to cry out to God. Asaph wrote, "When I was in distress, I sought the Lord; at night I stretched out untiring hands" (Psalm 77:2 NIV). Some nights, however, you may be *too* discouraged or troubled to pray. You may think that couldn't be, but it happens.

At times like that, instead of attempting to focus on a long prayer, shoot off short, sincere prayers every time you are able to focus, crying out for help. Quote faith-building verses. Sing hymns or songs of praise in your heart.

God will hear your prayers and answer, and after a while, the discouragement will dispel and sleep will return.

Lord, when sleep eludes me, I come to You. Show me what to do, whether it is to spend the time in prayer or to change something in my daily habits. Strengthen me for the day ahead so that I can do Your will. Amen.

Job Loss

Enduring Prolonged Unemployment

"Keep on asking, and you will receive what you ask for. Keep on seeking, and you will find."
MATTHEW 7:7 NLT

You may have been out of work so long that you have almost given up on finding employment. Or you may be working part-time for low wages. So you pray for God to change your situation. But when the drought continues, you may be tempted to give up.

In Elijah's day, Israel suffered from drought. After three and a half years, Elijah prayed for God to send rain. Then he told his servant to go look toward the sea. The servant returned, saying that he didn't see anything. Again Elijah prayed. Again he sent his servant. After doing this seven times, the servant finally saw a storm cloud.

Soon rain was falling heavily. The drought was over. But it didn't happen the first time Elijah prayed. He had to pray persistently before God answered (see 1 Kings 18:42–45). Jesus said that "men ought always to pray, and not to faint" (Luke 18:1 KJV).

So don't stop praying! You may have to wait awhile, but God will answer your prayers.

God, I am seeking, asking, and knocking again. I believe You will answer my prayer and make a way for me because Your Word tells me You will. In the meantime, give me strength to endure day by day. Amen.

Getting Fired

"What's this I hear about you? You're fired.
And I want a complete audit of your books."
LUKE 16:2 MSG

Jesus told a parable about a wasteful overseer whose misdeeds finally caught up with him. As a result, his boss fired him. This man had it coming, but you may have lost your job through no fault of your own. But if your boss thinks that you were wasteful or negligent, you could receive the same treatment as this manager.

Perhaps you were unintentionally careless with important details. Perhaps there was a major miscommunication and you lost a large account. Whatever happened, you suddenly find yourself out of work, and you realize that your boss is not going to be a good reference on your future job application.

At times like this, you have to stay positive and trust that God will provide for you and take care of your reputation. Life isn't always fair, and you won't always be treated the way you deserve. But if you refuse to focus on the wrong, you will get back on your feet much quicker. So "let the peace of God rule in your hearts" (Colossians 3:15 NKJV).

Lord, You are in control, and You know my situation. Help me
to not only focus on You as I look for a new job, but to also
be grateful for the blessings You have already given me. Help
me to forgive wrongs and keep moving forward. Amen.

Layoffs and Business Failures

"No craftsman of any craft shall be found in you anymore."
REVELATION 18:22 NKJV

You see it happening frequently these days: giant store chains suffer prolonged losses, and to staunch the bleeding, they cut thousands of jobs or close stores in cities across the nation. And these are sometimes businesses offering vital services and products.

This is a foretaste of the total economic crash of the final days. When Babylon the great, the worldwide commercial system, is destroyed, the Bible warns that "no craftsman of any craft shall be found in you anymore" (Revelation 18:22 NKJV). We see such breakdowns of basic services in war-torn nations and failed states today.

You may wonder how people survive such circumstances, but somehow they do—though to be sure, life is very difficult. But just such troubles have occurred many times before in earth's history, and God, knowing that they will happen again, promises to be with you.

He says, "Those who seek the LORD shall not lack any good thing" (Psalm 34:10 NKJV). It's important to trust God whether you are personally laid off or the world around you seems to be falling apart.

God, I cannot control the chaos around me. You are the one who is in control, so I will trust in You. Help me to be wise and focus on You as I wait patiently for answers to my prayers. Amen.

What Do I Do Now?

"Now what? My boss has fired me. I don't have the
strength to dig ditches, and I'm too proud to beg."
LUKE 16:3 NLT

Jesus told a parable about a rich man with vast wheat fields and olive orchards. One day he discovered that his manager was wasting his wealth. He fired him, of course.

The manager knew that word would quickly get out and no one would hire him as a manager. But this was the only skill he had. What could he do? Well, apparently there was a major irrigation project in the area. But ditch-digging was backbreaking work, and he was no longer young. His only other option was to beg, but that was too humiliating.

You may have lost a well-paying job due to a faltering economy, but you otherwise identify with the manager's question: "Now what?" You must either become a minimum-wage laborer or start panhandling. Even if you do have skills to fall back on, you may see a demotion in pay.

You will need courage and fortitude to make it through this difficult time of transition. Don't give up hope.

Father, give me courage and fortitude to face the challenges
in front of me. I need Your wisdom and strength to
move forward and make decisions for my future.
My only hope is in You, so I will not fear. Amen.

Job Stress

Work as unto the Lord

Work willingly at whatever you do, as though you
were working for the Lord rather than for people.
COLOSSIANS 3:23 NLT

One of the most common sources of stress on the job is having a boss you don't like. Some bosses seem to have the idea that since they are boss, they can be blunt and inconsiderate, and their workers have to put up with them or be put out the door. Even bosses who are more considerate and reasonable still may do things that irk you.

The Bible has a solution: if you can't change your boss' attitude, change your own. Work as if you are working for Jesus, not for imperfect people. Peter advised, "Submit yourselves to your masters, not only to those who are good and considerate, but also to those who are harsh" (1 Peter 2:18 NIV). He was writing this to slaves, and some had truly harsh masters.

For the last two thousand years, this advice has helped countless believers put up with unpleasant work—and not only survive, but thrive.

If you simply can't stand your boss, the best option might be to look for a new job.

Father, I will strive to do my best work so that I will honor
You, and I commit to pray for my boss and coworkers that
You will be at work in their lives and in the workplace.
Help me to be a faithful witness for You. Amen.

Intolerable Work Quotas

"Get your own straw wherever you can find it.
And not one brick less in your daily work quota!"
EXODUS 5:11 MSG

Some jobs have impossible work quotas. Workers may be expected to process a huge amount of units per day. In an effort to maximize profits and keep expenses down, many businesses try to squeeze as much work as possible out of their laborers for a minimum of pay.

They realize that quality is usually the first casualty of excessive work quotas, so they insist that you have to maintain quality no matter how much they pile on your plate. Either that or they give you the green light to produce substandard products.

Places of employment like that create constant stress, and while you can cope for a season, over time the situation will wear you down. You may have to stick with such a job for now to pay bills, but it is wise to keep your eyes open for alternate employment.

Pray that God gives you a better job with more reasonable expectations, and eventually the Lord will bring you out of "the house of bondage" (Exodus 13:14 NKJV).

God, strengthen me to withstand and persevere in this
difficult situation. I need deliverance from this bondage,
either through a reduction in what is required of me or a new
job. My expectation and hope lie in You alone. Amen.

A Heavy Workload

"We are unworthy servants who have simply done our duty."
LUKE 17:10 NLT

You shouldn't expect lavish praise for doing what you are paid to do. And while a good boss will comment when you do your job competently, he or she is not obliged to do so. Praise is only due when you go beyond the call of duty.

Where work stress can come in is when your boss regularly requires you to do more than your job description. If you protest, you may be told that many people would be happy to have your job. And that may be true.

You can carry the extra load for some time, but after a while the stress will get to you. Either that or you will need a fresh source of strength to buoy you up. That's where you must look to the Lord.

Jesus spoke to overworked laborers, saying, "Come unto me, all ye that labour and are heavy laden, and I will give you rest. Take my yoke upon you. . .and ye shall find rest unto your souls" (Matthew 11:28–29 KJV). Having spiritual peace can even help you carry a demanding workload.

Lord, I am weary and carrying a heavy burden. Sometimes I feel like I can't take anymore. I am coming to You because I need Your rest. Strengthen me and help me to persevere or send some relief, for without You I will fall. Amen.

Cheated out of Wages

The wages you failed to pay the workers who
mowed your fields are crying out against you.
JAMES 5:4 NIV

Have you ever been cheated out of money? Perhaps someone owed you for work you did but never paid the final installment. Or they paid you nothing at all. If you were depending on that income to pay bills, it may have left you in a tight situation and very stressed.

Israel had many day laborers. They needed to be paid at the end of each workday so that they could buy food. So the Bible warned employers, "Each day you shall give him his wages, . . .for he is poor and has set his heart on it; lest he cry out against you to the LORD, and it be sin to you" (Deuteronomy 24:15 NKJV).

God warned, "If. . .they cry at all to Me, I will surely hear their cry" (Exodus 22:23 NKJV). So rest assured: crooked employers won't forever get away with nonpayment. God can to do what is needed to get their attention. And if they don't respond in this life, they will have to answer for their actions in the next life.

God, You know I have been cheated of my wages,
and now bills are coming due that I can't pay because of
it. I need Your intervention. Help me to release any anger
and leave retribution and justice in Your hands. Amen.

Litigation

Settling out of Court

"When you are on the way to court with your adversary, settle your differences quickly."

MATTHEW 5:25 NLT

Even if you do your job conscientiously and well, things can go wrong. You might have a misunderstanding with a client, or perhaps your client has unreasonable expectations. But the next thing you know, your client is taking you to court or threatening to do so.

This can be stressful, especially if the person suing you is aggressive and is attacking your reputation and integrity. You can lose sleep, get stomach cramps from worry, or experience anxiety. At times like this, you must look to the Lord and trust Him to defend you.

If you can, settling out of court is best. You can often do this if you refuse to get ruffled and maintain a polite, professional attitude. Sometimes you must go the extra mile to show goodwill and make your client happy.

However, if the other person is simply unreasonable, you need to stand firm and refuse to be intimidated. Read Ezra 4–6 to see how the Jewish people defended their rights using a legal document when they were being strongly opposed.

Lord, give me wisdom in this situation. I want to behave in a way that honors You. Help me to remain calm and humble and try to settle the issue, but if my adversary is unreasonable, I ask for Your intervention. Amen.

A Place for Lawsuits

*"If there is imposed on him a sum of money,
then he shall pay. . .whatever is imposed on him."*

EXODUS 21:30 NKJV

Christians often seek to avoid litigation, even if they have a just cause, because of Paul's advice: "To have such lawsuits with one another is a defeat for you. Why not just accept the injustice and leave it at that?" (1 Corinthians 6:7 NLT).

But this refers to believers suing believers with unbelievers sitting in judgment, not to lawsuits in general. There are times to stand up for your legal rights and avoid someone gleefully cleaning you out. You have your family to provide for, after all. However, you should enter litigation prayerfully and judiciously.

And it works both ways. If someone does a careless job and you withhold payment until they finish it, they can take you to court—and things can get contentious. It's always best to try to reason with the other party and come to an agreement. There has to be some give-and-take.

As a believer, you are to be honest and just in your dealings. That doesn't include letting others rob you.

---

*Holy Spirit, I want to live in a way that is pleasing to
You, so I seek wisdom and guidance in dealing with this
issue. You know the situation. Help me to make choices
that will honor You and bring a good end. Amen.*

When Someone Sues You

*"If you are sued in court and your shirt is
taken from you, give your coat, too."*
MATTHEW 5:40 NLT

Jesus said that if someone sued you for the shirt off your back, you were to let him have your coat as well. In saying this, Jesus was acknowledging that sometimes believers would lose court cases, and He advised giving more than the law required to show that you are living undefeated and trusting God to care for you.

Some people protest that giving away so much would leave you destitute, so Jesus couldn't have meant to do this literally. But the point remains: the legal system isn't necessarily the "justice system," so instead of being defeated by injustices when they happen, you must live victoriously.

Under Roman law, Christians had their entire properties and possessions confiscated! The Bible says, "When *all you owned* was taken from you, you accepted it with joy. You knew there were better things waiting for you that will last forever" (Hebrews 10:34 NLT, emphasis added).

Even if you lose in man's courts, be encouraged, for "great is your reward in heaven" (Matthew 5:12 KJV).

---

*Father, I live in an unfair and wicked world, but You see
me and know my heart. I know You will make everything
right in the end, even if it is not what I desire. Help me
to have peace regardless of the outcome. Amen.*

Prodigal Children

When Children Go Astray

I have no greater joy than to hear that my children walk in truth.
3 JOHN 1:4 NKJV

John wrote that his greatest joy was to know that his children were serving the Lord. And that is true of countless Christian parents today. Seeing your children grow up and claim their faith as their own is immensely rewarding.

On the other hand, many parents live in grief because their children have gone astray despite everything they were taught. When they entered their teen years, they stopped listening to counsel and ceased going to church. And once they became adults, they became fully set in their own ways. This is heartbreaking, even if they are not into a wild lifestyle. If they have simply drifted away and show no interest in spiritual things, parents may feel as if they have failed. But the fact is, God has no grandchildren. Every generation must decide for themselves to love and obey God—or not.

The good news is, if parents are faithful to pray for their wayward children, God may yet work in their hearts and bring those children back to Himself.

Father, my children have strayed away from You even though I raised them in Your Word. You promised that if we trained them up in the truth, it would not return void, so I am trusting in You, and I leave them in Your hands. Amen.

Praying for Prodigals

*There is hope. . . , saith the L<small>ORD</small>, that thy
children shall come again to their own border.*
JEREMIAH 31:17 KJV

When the Jews' enemies, the Babylonians, invaded Judah, they took thousands of Jews prisoner to Babylon. Those who had been taken captive wept bitterly. "By the rivers of Babylon we sat and wept" (Psalm 137:1 NIV). And the Jews who had been left in Judah, many of them elderly, grieved for their relatives and children.

Many parents can identify with these emotions. When their children get caught up in lifestyles of partying, alcohol, drugs, and sexual immorality, they too have gone to the land of the enemy. So parents pray "that they may come to their senses and escape the snare of the devil, having been taken captive by him" (2 Timothy 2:26 NKJV).

Even if you pray earnestly with tears, you may have to pray for years, but God hears you. He finally told the Jews of old, "Refrain thy voice from weeping, and thine eyes from tears: for. . .they shall come again from the land of the enemy" (Jeremiah 31:16 KJV). And you can have this same hope today.

---

*God, I have wept for my children, but I still have hope
in You that one day they will return. Until then I will
continue to pray and trust in You. I am leaving them in
Your hands because You are my hope. Amen.*

Passive Rebellion

"Then the father told the other son, 'You go,'
and he said, 'Yes, sir, I will.' But he didn't go."
MATTHEW 21:30 NLT

Usually when you think of a prodigal, you think of a son or daughter living on his or her own and caught up in a wild lifestyle. But a prodigal can simply be someone whose heart is far from God, even when still living at home.

Jesus described two sons: when their father told one son to go work in the vineyard, he openly refused. The father then told his other son to go, and he replied, "Yes, sir, I will." But he didn't. He had only said yes to get his father off his back. Had he actually gone to the vineyard, he would have done a lazy, careless job.

Many backslidden teens go to church and talk the "God talk," but they are merely going through the motions. They appear to be good Christians, but as one writer confessed, "I was almost in all evil in the midst of the congregation" (Proverbs 5:14 KJV). You need to pray for such prodigals as much as for the openly rebellious ones. God can change them too.

Holy Spirit, please work in the spirit of my child to bring
them from just going through the motions to a dedicated
walk with You. May their yes be yes, and may their no be no.
Help them to have a solid commitment to You. Amen.

Turning from Ruin

Repent, and turn yourselves from all your transgressions;
so iniquity shall not be your ruin.
EZEKIEL 18:30 KJV

It hurts you to see one of your children go astray and make the classical mistakes of youth. You are aware from your own experience and the experience of others of the price tag of a wild, disobedient lifestyle. It can utterly derail and ruin them.

You want to spare your children such a fate, so you warn them, you try to explain to them, but if they don't listen, all you can do is pray for them.

Let them know that although you disagree with their choices, you will always love them unconditionally, just like the father of the prodigal son (Luke 15:20–24). When they are ready to change, they will turn to the person who accepts them, not judges them.

Some people apparently need to hit rock bottom, to experience utter ruin, before they are willing to seek help. But pray that God will get you through to your children before that point. If they repent and turn from their willful ways, they can avoid the road to ruin. And many youth do.

Father, I ask You to be at work in my child's life. Help them to see
the truth of their situation and return to You. Give me the words
to speak and the wisdom to know when to be silent. Amen.

Sickness

Staying Healthy

*Some of you were sick because you'd lived a bad life,
your bodies feeling the effects of your sin.*
PSALM 107:17 MSG

Some people believe that all illnesses are caused by sin. If they suffer a stomach ailment, it is because they failed to tithe. If they have arthritis, it is because they spoke unkindly to someone. Certainly medical conditions can have spiritual and psychosomatic roots. However, people bring many sicknesses on themselves by their lifestyle choices. Those who overeat and don't exercise are at a high risk of heart disease. People who have a steady diet of junk food are prone to plugged arteries and a plethora of other illnesses. And if they abuse their bodies with alcohol or tobacco, they are in danger of liver disease and cancer, respectively.

God has set up this physical world to operate according to very practical rules. Violate those rules and you will bring trouble upon yourself. "You realize, don't you, that you are the temple of God. . . ? No one will get by with vandalizing God's temple, you can be sure of that" (1 Corinthians 3:16–17 MSG). Take care of your body. You will be glad you did.

Lord, my body is Your temple, so help me to treat it with respect by eating better and exercising so that I am more able to do Your will in my life. Help me to be the best that I can be to honor You. Amen.

God Restores Your Health

*Whenever we're sick and in bed, G*OD *becomes*
our nurse, nurses us back to health.

PSALM 41:3 MSG

God often heals His children, but we frequently take it for granted. Think of the powers of healing God has given your body. Time and again when you are sick or injured, your body is restored to health. Each time it happens, it is a miracle of His creative power. And many times when a sickness or injury is beyond your body's ability to heal, God supernaturally intervenes and reaches out to mend you.

Some Christians believe that the New Testament's emphasis on healing is a thing of the past, while others believe that Christians today can still lay claim to healing. God is still God, and He can and does heal.

"[God] forgives all your iniquities [and] heals all your diseases" (Psalm 103:3 NKJV). God still forgives all your sins, and there is no reason that He can't still heal. Of course, He doesn't act every time you want Him to, and He may allow you to be sick for quite some time. But you can be thankful for the times He does heal.

God, thank You for being faithful to forgive me and to
heal me, physically and spiritually. I praise You when
relief is quick to come, and I pray for strength to persevere
when healing takes longer if it is Your will. Amen.

Protected from Illness

"You must serve only the LORD your God.
If you do, . . .I will protect you from illness."
EXODUS 23:25 NLT

God has made many promises in His Word to heal sickness and to protect you from getting sick. This verse explains one of the main conditions—you must wholeheartedly serve God.

You may wonder, *Doesn't Mark 11:24 say that all I need is faith? If I have enough faith I'll receive whatever I ask for—including protection from illness.* Certainly you do need faith, but there are conditions. The apostle John wrote, "Whatsoever we ask, we receive of him, because we keep his commandments, and do those things that are pleasing in his sight" (1 John 3:22 KJV).

It's a lot better to be obedient and avoid getting sick in the first place than it is to get sick and need healing. And much of staying healthy comes from obeying simple, commonsense rules, such as eating healthily.

You may still get sick from time to time, even if you are obedient, but God has promised, "Many are the afflictions of the righteous, but the LORD delivers him out of them all" (Psalm 34:19 NKJV).

Father, I seek to be obedient and live a healthy lifestyle,
but sometimes I falter and fall, and sometimes illness
is just a result of this world. Give me the strength to
endure and for healing if it be Your will. Amen.

Unforgiveness
Reasons to Forgive

*"If you do not forgive others their sins,
your Father will not forgive your sins."*

MATTHEW 6:15 NIV

When someone deliberately offends you, takes advantage of you, gossips about you, or harms you, God understands how hurt you feel. He also knows that it is a common reaction to want the other person to feel pain in return.

But only God can administer justice perfectly. So the Bible says, "Do not take revenge, my dear friends, but leave room for God's wrath, for it is written: 'It is mine to avenge; I will repay,' says the Lord" (Romans 12:19 NIV). Not taking matters into your own hands but instead trusting God to make things right takes faith.

God is well able to do that, but He needs you to unhook your fingers from the offense and give Him room to work. He even needs you to refrain from praying for vengeance and to forgive the offending party. After all, you have committed offenses yourself. "LORD, if you kept a record of our sins, who, O Lord, could ever survive?" (Psalm 130:3 NLT).

God forgives you. . .if you forgive others.

---

*Lord, I don't want to be trapped by unforgiveness. Help me to forgive
and let go of the offense. I give the person to You to do as You see
fit. Help me to move on without looking back anymore. Amen.*

A Reason to Forgive

*Be ye kind one to another, tenderhearted, forgiving one
another, even as God for Christ's sake hath forgiven you.*
EPHESIANS 4:32 KJV

God forgave all your sins, not because you deserved it—you didn't—
but because of Christ's death on the cross.

For this reason, the Bible says that you also should forgive others
who have hurt or offended you. Again, you don't do this because
these people *deserve* to be forgiven—they may not—but because
you are motivated by love. "For the love of Christ compels us"
(2 Corinthians 5:14 NKJV). You are to forgive others the same way
that God forgave you.

God is aware when others maliciously hurt you or use you, and
He is not saying that what they do should simply be excused or
overlooked because they are only human. But what He does ask you
to do is to forgive—even though they are guilty.

You should especially be tenderhearted toward fellow Christians.
You are to live in love, "forgiving one another, if anyone has a complaint against another; even as Christ forgave you, so you also must
do" (Colossians 3:13 NKJV). If you do this, God will bless you richly.

---

*Jesus, You loved me enough to die on the cross so that You could
offer forgiveness for sins. If You have forgiven me, then I must forgive
those who have hurt me, but I need Your help to let it go. Amen.*

Forgiveness Is Serious Business

"This is how my heavenly Father will treat each of you
unless you forgive your brother or sister from your heart."
MATTHEW 18:35 NIV

God knows that if you have been deeply offended or wounded, it takes time to process the pain, release it to Him, and forgive the person who hurt you. But in the end, you must forgive.

Jesus told a parable about a master who forgave his servant an enormous debt. However, the servant then seized a fellow servant who owed him a small sum and threw him in jail. Angrily, the master asked, "Shouldn't you have had mercy on your fellow servant just as I had on you?" (Matthew 18:33 NIV). Then he ordered the first servant to be afflicted in prison.

Jesus warned that God would treat believers the same way if they didn't forgive others. You must forgive others who have offended you, knowing that you yourself have been forgiven for many offenses.

God has had great mercy on you and continues to shower you with compassion. If you are filled with His love and are walking in His Spirit, you will love those who have offended you. . .and show them mercy as well.

Father, I am struggling to forgive, but I know I can't hold on to
unforgiveness when I have been forgiven for so much. Help me to
forgive and let go, not only for their sake but for my own. Amen.

Why We Must Forgive

You may not feel a need to forgive others, but when you are in need of forgiveness, you are desperate for God to forgive. But there is a catch: in essence, Jesus said you should pray, "Forgive us our sins the exact same way we have forgiven those who have sinned against us."

But what if you have refused to forgive those indebted to you, who have sinned against you? The answer is clear: if you haven't forgiven others, then God is under no obligation to forgive you either. And He won't.

Some people think this is unfair. They think God should forgive them their many trespasses no matter how much bitterness and rage they have in their heart against His children. But should God forgive you if you have bitterness and anger against Him? No. "Whoever does not love their brother and sister, whom they have seen, cannot love God, whom they have not seen" (1 John 4:20 NIV). If you don't love others and forgive them, you don't love God, and God won't forgive you if you hate Him.

Lord, You are just and faithful and no respecter of persons, so what You require of one, You require of all. I know I have to forgive others if I want to be forgiven by You, so teach me how to let go. Amen.

Violence

Avoiding Violence

The answer's simple: Live right, speak the truth, . . .reject violence.
ISAIAH 33:15–16 MSG

When someone cuts you off in traffic, nearly causing an accident, you are understandably angry. The same is true when someone physically attacks you, vandalizes your property, or lies about you. Anger has its rightful place, but the Bible warns, "Be angry, and do not sin" (Ephesians 4:26 NKJV). Many people sin when they are angry by committing violent acts against others.

Violence can quickly spiral out of control; you might hurt someone more than you intended to, and end up facing serious consequences. Plus, violence usually provokes more violence and vendettas; you create bitter enemies, and you too can end up hurt.

Psalm 7:16 (NIV) says, "The trouble they cause recoils on them; their violence comes down on their own heads." Violence is almost always a two-edged sword, hurting those who strike out as much as those they attack.

If you must take some form of action to protect yourself, be aware that there are a number of well-thought-out responses that avoid violence. Even when exercising your right to self-defense, use restraint.

God, we live in a violent and wicked world, but we are supposed to be a light in the darkness. Help me to take the high road and be angry, but sin not. Give me wisdom and protection so that I can avoid violence if possible. Amen.

Living by the Sword

"Put away your sword," Jesus told him.
"Those who use the sword will die by the sword."
MATTHEW 26:52 NLT

Many criminals live by the sword. They pack heavy firepower, sometimes even outgunning the police. They live and die in a violent world. But many people today engage in violence, even though they don't use guns. They give vent to their anger with their fists or whatever objects they can get ahold of.

If you find yourself expressing anger with violence, seek help to manage your temper. You may have avoided doing damage thus far, but it is only a matter of time before you do something that you will regret. You may traumatize loved ones, and though you apologize afterward, the damage will have been done.

Violence will also get you in trouble with the law. Eventually, failing to curb your temper will ensure that you suffer at the hands of another violent person. If you use the sword, you will die by the sword. It will take time, but it will certainly happen.

Trust God to work out situations, and turn away from violence. This will give God the needed space to work.

Lord, teach me to keep a cool head and remember the dangers
of a violent temper. I trust You to help me to handle my situation,
but I need You to work in my spirit to remove the anger
before it costs me more than I am willing to pay. Amen.

A Violent World

The earth also was corrupt before God,
and the earth was filled with violence.
GENESIS 6:11 NKJV

In Noah's day the earth was a very violent place, and Jesus tells us that "as the days of Noah were, so also will the coming of the Son of Man be" (Matthew 24:37 NKJV).

Every time you watch the news, you see incidents of violence. There is a steady stream of crime in the streets, in the malls, in the schools, and in the homes of our nation. You get the impression that the hour is late for planet Earth.

But all this violence isn't just a statistic, nor is it simply a fulfill-ment of Bible prophecy; real crimes are being committed against real people. You yourself or a member of your family may have been a victim of violent crime and know the trauma it brings. It can leave you shaken and insecure.

But know this also: "God has not given us a spirit of fear, but of power and of love," and "perfect love casts out fear" (2 Timothy 1:7; 1 John 4:18 NKJV). So let God fill you with His assurance and love.

Father, the world is filled with violence, but You have not
given us a spirit of fear. You have given us a spirit of
power and love because perfect love casts out fear.
Fill me with that spirit of power and love. Amen.

Worry

Give God Your Worries

Give all your worries and cares to God, for he cares about you.
1 PETER 5:7 NLT

Everyone worries from time to time, but some people are especially prone to it. Whichever category you fall into—but especially if you are a constant worrier—God's solution is to give Him all your cares. Why? Because a constant state of anxiety isn't good for your mental or physical health. Psalm 37:8 (NKJV) says, "Do not fret—it only causes harm."

There are two more reasons why you should hand all your worries and cares to God. The first is that He genuinely cares about you and doesn't want you to suffer needlessly. Knowing the human tendency to want to try to sort everything out, He made it a command: "Give all your worries and cares to God."

The second reason is that God is all-powerful and is, in fact, the only one in existence capable of resolving all your problems.

"Let us therefore come boldly unto the throne of grace," lay the problem at His feet, and trust Him to "help in time of need" (Hebrews 4:16 KJV).

God, I come boldly to Your throne. I know You are the only one who can handle my situation. Worrying about it will make me weak and sick, so I am bringing my worries to Your throne to leave at Your feet. Amen.

Worrying Is Useless

"Can any one of you by worrying add a single hour to your life?"
MATTHEW 6:27 NIV

Not only can you not add one hour to your life by worrying, but worry will probably cut years from your life. Anxiety, prolonged over time, has a negative effect on your health, leading to insomnia, stomach disorders, and—in worst-case scenarios—heart attacks.

Jesus warned that stress would be a major killer in the last days, with "men's hearts failing them from fear" (Luke 21:26 NKJV). So worrying is not only useless but worse than useless. . .and highly detrimental.

So many people worry about trivial things, yet Jesus admonished you not even to worry about vitally important things. He said, "Therefore do not worry, saying, 'What shall we eat?' or 'What shall we drink?' or 'What shall we wear?' " (Matthew 6:31 NKJV).

Certainly God expects you to work to provide the money you need to live, so He is not advising you to be lazy or complacent. But He commands you not to worry. Even if your financial situation is unstable, you do well to remember that God is your ultimate provider.

Father, worry is not good for anything except as a weapon of the enemy. Your Word tells me not to worry but to trust You to provide for all my needs, so I am asking for Your provision and peace. Amen.

One Day at a Time

"Do not worry about tomorrow, for tomorrow will worry about itself. Each day has enough trouble of its own."
MATTHEW 6:34 NIV

Jesus warned against the futility of worrying about the future, focusing on trouble that hasn't even happened yet. Doing so distracts you from important things you should concentrate on today.

Certainly if there are large events or problems looming on the horizon—for example, if you are responsible for organizing a banquet—you can't ignore giving thought to them. But you are simply to make whatever plans you can then commit the unresolved details to God in prayer, not worry about them.

The difference between *planning for* tomorrow and *worrying about* tomorrow is that worrying often involves getting your eyes on the entire problem at once then despairing that you can't handle it, whereas planning means having the faith that you can meet the challenge if you pray and take practical steps to meet it.

When Jesus said that today already has enough troubles that require your attention, He was basically advising you to keep your eyes on God, moment by moment, not on your problems.

Lord, as I make plans for the future, I know that problems can arise to get in the way. I trust You'll help me to work through them rather than to worry needlessly over them. Help me to keep my eyes on You instead of the problems. Amen.

Worry Weighs You Down

Worry weighs us down; a cheerful word picks us up.
PROVERBS 12:25 MSG

If you are concerned about your finances, your health, a wayward child, a relationship, or any number of other things, you will be tempted to worry. This is especially true if the situation looks difficult and things stand a very real chance of not working out in your favor.

At times like that, a cheerful word can encourage you. It doesn't even have to be the total solution to your problems, such as, "The check just arrived!" or "The test came back negative!" It can simply be a cheerful word, someone letting you know that he or she cares—because that lets you know that *God* cares.

The reason this can be so encouraging is that although you would like God to resolve things at once, your immediate need is to know that God sees your situation, cares, and will be coming through for you. This is why David prayed, "Send me a sign of your favor. . . . For you, O LORD, help and comfort me" (Psalm 86:17 NLT).

This is also a good reason to be sure to comfort and encourage others.

---

*God, I need a word of encouragement today because
life is hard, and I need to know You hear me. However,
help me to be open to opportunities to share a word of
encouragement to those I meet as well. Amen.*

Scripture Index

OLD TESTAMENT

GENESIS

6:11	182
23:2	64
24:67	61
25:8	111
30:1	152
30:14	93
35:29	60
37:4	96

EXODUS

4:11	75
5:11	163
20:14	22
21:30	167
23:25	175

LEVITICUS

21:18	73
26:36	129

NUMBERS

14:41	116

DEUTERONOMY

26:6	8
31:6	130

JOSHUA

2:9	148
7:21	146

JUDGES

11:2	119
16:15	88

RUTH

1:3	63
1:20–21	37

1 SAMUEL

1:6–7	97
1:11	153
17:28–29	120

2 SAMUEL

4:4	71
12:22–23	55

1 KINGS

1:6	100
17:17	56

2 KINGS

1:2	11
4:1	36
6:33	131
17:39	108

2 CHRONICLES

16:12	54
19:7	81
20:12	44

JOB

5:26	62
6:11	67
6:13	141
6:17–18	77
6:20	78

9:28 150
16:22 110
17:5 42
30:6 137
31:1 16

PSALMS

4:8 156
10:17 140
12:5 142
25:19 105
35:14 59
41:3 174
41:7 107
41:8 52
41:9 40
48:14 112
56:1 45
56:2 106
56:3 127
73:25 154
77:4 157
78:32–33 114
91:12 13
102:4 68
107:17 173
109:11 38
112:7 128
124:2–3 46
127:2 34
129:2 48
139:23–24 144

PROVERBS

3:24 155
5:10 117
6:16, 19 121
6:32 19
11:3 82
11:13 41
12:25 186
13:11 85
13:12 76
14:29 31
16:31 102
17:18 134
18:14 69
19:11 32
19:19 15
20:1 25
21:17 18
23:22 103
23:29–30 24
28:13 145
29:22 30

ECCLESIASTES

2:22–23 33
7:9 28
9:12 12
10:9 10

ISAIAH

5:11 27
5:22 26
7:9 92
16:2 138

33:15–16 180	**HOSEA**
40:11 6	7:4, 7 23
40:27 147	**JOEL**
49:4 115	2:25 39
54:6 86	**MICAH**
54:11, 14 7	2:9 9
65:20 58	7:6 99
JEREMIAH	**HAGGAI**
10:19 53	1:9 80
12:6 98	**ZECHARIAH**
31:17 170	8:4 104
39:17 109	8:6 151
EZEKIEL	
18:30 172	
24:16 65	

NEW TESTAMENT

MATTHEW	26:52 181
5:25 166	**MARK**
5:28 20	5:26 50
5:40 168	8:24 74
6:12 179	**LUKE**
6:15 176	8:52 57
6:25 133	10:40 122
6:27 184	13:4 14
6:34 185	14:13–14 72
7:7 158	16:2 159
18:35 178	16:3 161
20:12 123	16:10 83
21:30 171	16:22 113
24:10 43	

17:10 164
24:38 89

JOHN
4:18 87
5:5 51
12:37 90

ACTS
14:22 49
15:39 118

ROMANS
5:5 79

1 CORINTHIANS
3:17 94
4:11 136

2 CORINTHIANS
1:8 47
4:8 66
8:13 135

EPHESIANS
4:17 149
4:32 177
6:4 125

PHILIPPIANS
2:21 126
4:13 139
4:14 70
4:6 35

COLOSSIANS
3:23 162

1 TIMOTHY
5:4 101
5:8 124

TITUS
2:9–10 84

HEBREWS
11:6 91
11:34 143

JAMES
1:19 29
5:4 165

1 PETER
5:7 183

2 PETER
2:14 21
2:22 17

3 JOHN
1:4 169

REVELATION
6:6 132
9:21 95
18:22 160